I0022860

Anchored

in The Word & Sponsored by Grace:

The Sustaining Power of Word and Grace Synergy

by
U. E. David MBA, MDiv.

Copyright 2024 Udoh E. David MBA, MDiv. All rights reserved.

ISBN- 979-8-9899727-2-2

No part of this book may be reproduced in any form or by any electronic or mechanical means including information storage and retrieval systems. from the author. The only exception is by a reviewer, who may. quote, and short excerpts in a review.

Trade Culture Press Books may be ordered from the major booksellers near you or on-line. Although the author and publisher have made every effort to ensure that the information in this book was correct at press time, the author and publisher do not assume and, at this moment, disclaim any liability to any party for any loss, damage, or disruption caused by errors or omissions, whether such errors or omissions result from negligence, accident, or any other cause. This publication is designed to provide accurate and authoritative information about the subject matter covered. It is sold with the understanding that the publisher does not render professional services. If legal advice or other expert assistance is required, the services of a competent professional should be sought. The fact that an organization or website is referred to in this work as a citation and/or a potential source of further information does not mean that the author or the publisher endorses the information the organization or website may provide or recommendations it may make.

Please remember that Internet websites listed in this work may have changed or

disappeared between when this work was written and when it was read.

All the images depicted are provided by stock photos, and such images used are authorized for illustrative purposes.

Dedication

All praise and glory be to God, the Almighty, who is the wellspring of every good and perfect idea. To my spiritual sons and daughters. My immediate and extended family. To everyone called to the ministry and the Apostolic calling, I am encouraging you to seek out the sacred meeting place of God's Word and His limitless grace, shedding light on the mutually beneficial relationship between the two and the life-altering potential they possess for you as a believer navigating the unpredictable terrain of this world.
The upcoming days will be better.

Acknowledgment

This book, "Anchored in the Word and Sponsored by Grace," to the body of Christ, is meant to be an encouragement and spiritual guide, motivating readers that no matter the uncertainty, one must have holy trust. God's Word is a steadfast lifeline.

I want to thank everyone who made this project possible, my beloved church and family, Gospel House Revival Ministries (GHRM), for your constant support, prayers, and encouragement in writing this book. You have been an unreplaceable source of strength and inspiration. You've also fueled my desire to propagate God's message regarding love and steadfastness.

To my lovely Children and my Beautiful wife, Prophetess Ayi, who has always been that strength and continuous source of inspiration in the temple of our hearts. Your faith in me, patience, love, and steadfast belief have been the foundation for this book's development. Your support and encouragement are no less important than my parents' blessings. I am ever blessed for your love – I Love you more.

I would also like to thank the publishers of this book for running it. Everything throughout the process was beyond value because of your expertise and devoted support. First of all, your focus on excellence and dedication to promoting the distribution of spiritual literature is commendable. I am thankful for this collaboration with a recognized publishing team like yours.

To future readers of "Anchored in the Word and Sponsored by Grace," this is my sincere remark: It is my heartfelt wish that the words presented in these pages not only touch your hearts deeply but also inspire you to believe truthfully and trustingly in the fundamental promises by God. May you find comfort, strength, and a Godly direction through all the trials of life as so often it seems to be a journey and darkness with an unknown ending, but no, there is dependable truth, and it is God's Word.

Finally, I would like to thank all those who have been my well-wishers and supporters from the beginning of this journey. An unwavering belief in this message affirms your words of encouragement and prayers. I want to convey that these years have helped me and played a significant role in my service. The support you have given me has increased my sense of meaning and motivation to pass on God's words and transformative power to many more out there.

Finishing my statement, I am humbled by all the efforts made. I appreciate everyone coming together to make it possible to finalize this work, "Anchored in the Word and Sponsored by Grace." May this book be a source of hope and help the faith of those who read it firmly while making them grow in their appreciation for God's love that never falters or fails. We are counting on the faithfulness of God Almighty.

With deepest gratitude,

Apostle, David Udoh, MBA, MDiv

Executive President

Gospel House Revival Ministries

www.ghrmusa.org

Table of Contents

Introduction

In this age where uncertainty often clouds the horizon of our lives, an anchor becomes an indispensable symbol of stability and strength. The power of the Word and the indelible touch of Grace in a Christian's walk stand as twin beacons lighting the path ahead—each step at once an encounter with the divine and a journey of self-discovery. This book is conceived with a heartfelt purpose to provide practical insights that enable us to find robust frameworks from the Scriptures and forge a life of unwavering faith and confidence. As we turn its pages, you are invited to undertake a transformative mission that would help you absorb and reflect the depths of God's Grace, share these treasures with others, and spend your days with ease in calm or stormy times, undergoing an experience marked by transformation.

Models of an anchor are profoundly significant in today's era, which is riddled with unpredictability; the imagery stands for the stability and strength that our lives crave amid their always-changing landscape. "Anchored in the Word and Sponsored by Grace" is not just a book but an invitation from the heart to plunge into that sacred journey of spiritual growth and steadfast faith. It is rich in insights that will help us firmly establish ourselves in the truths of Scripture, strengthening a life marked by steadfast belief and unwavering conviction.

This book is designed to serve as a beacon of light, revealing the strong connection between God's living Word and His unbounded

Grace—an all-embracing favor supporting our journey. Let this be a profound and life-changing journey as you turn these pages. Open up your soul for the brightness of God's Grace and resolve to share this priceless spiritual treasure with all you meet. Let the figure of God's Grace illuminate your heart and do everything to reach out and provide this priceless spiritual treasure for others.

Take this piece as an ever-present friend during peaceful and stormy seasons. It intends to illuminate us toward a more profound knowledge of divine Grace by providing intimate insight into engagements with the Word of God and the essence of His Grace. This publication guides you through self-discovery and divine encounters to understand God's heart, grasp His Grace, and live out your faith. It is an inspiring torch on your inner journey, a treasure trove for individual development, and an urgent message to practice what God has called you into—strength in our changing world. "Anchored in the Word and Sponsored by Grace" is much more than a book; it extends past its cover pages to be an earnest way of inviting individuals into their spiritual maturity and continuous faith.

Like a constant friend, "Anchored in the Word and Sponsored by Grace" is set against two different times – calm and stormy. It is focused on the Grace abundant enough to validate us all together as we move forward. This book will lead you through self-discovery and divine encounters to help guide you. This work stands as an encouraging lantern on your spiritual odyssey, a rich repository for personal improvement, and the clarion call to step out in boldness of purpose according to God's design.

The Power of the Word and Grace in a Christian's Life

In the unfurling canvas of a Christian's life, nothing wields more transformative power than the marriage of God's Word with His overflowing grace. Let's delve into how these twin pillars uphold our daily walk and sculpt our faith.

The Word is a beacon, guiding the believer through life's tumultuous seas. In essence, it is the very breath of God, captured in the text, alive and vibrant. Scriptures are not merely words to be read but food for the soul and a lamp unto the feet. To engage with the Word is to engage with the Divine Himself, allowing His truths to infiltrate the heart and mind.

Simultaneously, grace emerges like a gentle dawn after the darkest nights, a reminder that God's love is unearned, boundless, and perpetual. This grace is the undercurrent that carries the believer, teaching us that our salvation and every good thing we experience is a gift, not a wage for deeds done.

When the Word imbued with Spirit enters the heart, it is like a seed planted in fertile soil. It requires the water of grace to germinate, grow, and eventually yield abundant fruit. This fruit manifests in many ways; it strengthens character, influences decisions, and pours love toward others.

It's paramount to recognize that immersion in Scripture without acknowledging grace can lead to legalism, while dwelling on grace without the foundation of the Word may yield a directionless faith. Together, they form the plumb line against which all actions and thoughts are measured.

Consider the gentle conviction that sweeps over one when reading passages highlighting human nature's shortfall. This is the Word at work, not to condemn but to correct. Yet, grace whispers the promise of forgiveness, empowerment, and hope, assuring the heart of the Father's unfailing love.

As the Word illuminates the path, grace empowers Christians to walk it. In moments of weakness, when the flesh crumbles, grace stands as the scaffold, holding the believer up and providing strength to persevere. In this divine enabling, the true power of grace is most palpable, turning human weakness into displays of God's glory.

God's grace and His Word are particularly poignant in instances of repentance. When one stumbles and falls into sin, the Word is there to convict, to show the fault line. Yet, grace is the hand that lifts the transgressor, cleansing and setting them back on the righteous path with renewed purpose.

In the daily grind, too, this duo proves to be indispensable. The world's noises grow faint as the Scripture speaks; its timeless wisdom cuts through confusion, offering clear direction. And in every small success and minor victory, grace humbles, reminding the believer that every perfect gift descends from above.

Community life within the Body of Christ further underscores the necessity of grace and the Word. Harmony among believers flows from scriptural mandates to love and serve one another, while grace covers the inevitable frictions, fostering forgiveness and unity.

The transformative effects of these elements cannot be overstated. As the Word renews the mind, grace transforms the heart. Together, they produce a believer who knows about God and emulates His character, embodying love, patience, kindness, and all the fruits that the Spirit yields.

Moreover, in the context of mission and evangelism, the Word equips believers with the message of the Gospel, while grace softens the soil of the listener's heart, making way for seeds of truth to take root. Witnessing becomes less of an obligatory task and more of a natural overflow of a lifestyle steeped in Scripture and grace.

Lastly, in the inevitable approach of life's winter seasons, the Word and grace stand like a formidable fortress against despair. The scriptures provide the promises that anchor hope, while grace ensures that these promises are not just ideals but accessible realities to the weary heart.

A Christian's life is marked by growth and maturity through reading, meditating, and living out the Word, hand in hand with a constant reliance on grace. This symbiotic relationship between God's spoken truth and his divine kindness is the foundation upon which believers can not only stand but flourish, facing the future with unwavering faith and unshakeable confidence.

Thus, the power of the Word and grace is life-altering potency and necessity to all who would receive and apply them. They are the twin stars by which Christians navigate, the forces that shape their destinies, and the very essence of their identity in Christ.

The Purpose of the Book

Having pondered the profound influence that the Word and grace have in the fabric of a Christian's life, we turn now to our core question: why write this book? Let's begin by saying that this work is crafted as a guide that seeks to provide readers with practical insights and establish a firm foundation in Scripture.

The intent is straightforward yet profound—to help readers navigate life's inevitable challenges with unwavering faith and confidence. This very conviction compels someone to rise after a fall, the invisible foundation upon which character is built and resilience is fostered.

Throughout this narrative, the objective remains to grasp and unfold the infinite concepts of divine grace. We aim to delve into the richness of God's undeserved favor toward humanity and articulate how this grace, when properly understood, can transform lives.

The journey we embark upon is intended to be one of shared discoveries and encouragement, leading to the metamorphosis of our inner beings. As our compass, we'll employ the timeless wisdom embedded within Scripture. Its truths are not relics of a bygone era but evergreen principles that guide our daily living.

Witnessing to others means sharing this rich tapestry of grace and truth we are unraveling. In our sharing, there is multiplication—not just of knowledge, but of the profound joy of walking with the Divine. One's journey of faith is never solely for personal improvement; it ripples outward, impacting lives we may never directly touch.

Fundamentally, this book aims to beckon readers to live transformed, to allow the principles contained within these pages to inform and reform—from thought to action, from belief to behavior. Transformation is not an immediate spectacle but a gradual illumination of the heart and mind.

A unique blend of instructional wisdom, compassionate counsel, and Scriptural insights awaits you. In the tradition of great writers who have wed the profound with the practical, we strive to provide a narrative that speaks not just to the mind but also to the heart's deepest yearnings.

While the journey through the text will undoubtedly confront you with the profound mysteries of grace and the solidity of God's Word, it also promises a simplicity necessary for daily application. The Word is more than literature; it is a living interaction that continually ignites the path before us.

The road to understanding grace and applying the Word has its hurdles. This book recognizes such difficulties, directing attention to overcoming these barriers through genuine examples and actionable steps. Resilience, after all, is fostered not by avoiding challenges but by facing and mastering them.

As we journey from topic to topic, the core mission is always to bring us back to the center—back to the reality of God's love and the transformative power he offers through his Word and grace. Reflections on these truths aim not merely for intellectual ascent but for the resonance of the soul.

This work, which rests in your hands, is an invitation—an invitation to explore, question, wrestle with, and ultimately embrace the truths of Scripture and the complexities of grace. Pursuing this knowledge is intertwined with a fuller, more prosperous life rooted in the eternal.

Only when the truths of grace and the reliability of Scripture permeate our very being can we confidently say we lead a life anchored and sponsored by the divine. This is the life this book endeavors to lead you towards—a life of certainty amid storms, hope when faced with despair, and love in the presence of indifference.

With every chapter and each page turned the aim is to encourage spiritual growth and grit in grace. It offers assurance that, despite our human frailty, there is a strength available that far surpasses all understanding—a strength that equips us for every good work and challenge.

In conclusion, the introduction to purpose reminds us that the goal isn't to finish first or claim victory by merit. The goal is to journey well—to learn, grow, and become beacons of grace and truth, fully alive in a world that desperately needs the light we carry.

May this book serve as your companion in the venture of faith, illuminating the steps before you and guiding you into the deep, boundless ocean of God's grace, where assurance and peace abound, and life is lived to its most whole measure, anchored by the Word.

Overview of the Structure of this book

In navigating the waters of spiritual growth, it's essential to have a keen understanding of the vessel that carries us. This book has been crafted as a sequence of words and a structured journey, a blueprint for delving deeply into the transformative power of grace and the guiding light of the Word of God. In this part of our introduction, we will consider the overarching framework of the book, laying out the design that holds the content in place and drawing the roadmap for our exploration.

The subsequent chapters act as building blocks, commencing with Chapter 1: 'The Foundation of Our Faith,' which delves into the critical concepts of grace and the importance of the Word in our lives. Here, we dissect the essence of grace and scrutinize the role of Scripture not only as a revelation of divine truth but also as our steadfast spiritual anchor in a turbulent world.

Moving forward, Chapter 2: 'Grace as a Divine Sponsor' unpacks the concept of unmerited favor and its transformative effects on the human heart and soul. This chapter also highlights the symbiotic relationship between grace and faith, providing insight into how faith actively responds to the presence of grace in our lives.

Chapter 3: 'Anchored in the Word' calls us to recognize the Bible as our spiritual compass. Through an exploration of Scripture's infallibility and sufficiency, this section offers practical advice for nurturing a profound connection with God's Word amidst life's challenges.

In Chapter 4: 'Grace and Transformation,' we delve into how God powers the journey toward holiness and sanctification and how the

Word is a vital tool for spiritual growth and applying divine principles in our daily existence.

The role of grace within our interpersonal relationships is explored in Chapter 5: 'Grace and Relationships,' which illustrates how grace influences forgiveness and guides us in our interactions with others, in line with biblical principles of love and compassion.

Life's disruptions are addressed in Chapter 6: 'Anchored in the Storm,' offering strategies,' or navigating life's challenges through grace, and turning to the Word for comfort and resilience during seasons of adversity and trial.

Chapter 7: 'Sharing Grace and the Word' explores our call to mission, discussing what it means to spread the Gospel of grace and to be equipped by Scripture for effective witness and ambassadorship in a world that thirsts for truth.

As believers pursue a life firmly rooted in divine truth and love, Chapter 8: 'Living a Life Anchored in the Word and Sponsored by Grace' presents the journey of transformation and the call to persist in abiding within the realms of God's Word and grace.

The theme of community is embraced in Chapter 9: 'Embracing Community through Grace,' underlining the importance of forming a supportive network of believers who encourage one another in the faith.

'Grace in Service and Ministry,' the focal point of Chapter 10, discusses serving with humility and the diverse expressions of service that emanate from the body of Christ, each member working in tandem with the gifts bestowed upon them.

Chapter 11: 'The Discipline of Gratitude' shifts our gaze towards maintaining a spirit of thankfulness, encouraging a posture of gratitude as we recognize the daily manifestations of grace in our lives.

In Chapter 12: 'The Leadership of the Word,' we explore the Biblical foundation for leadership and how to navigate the delicate balance of walking in authority clothed in humility.

With our sights lifted heavenward, Chapter 13: 'The Horizon of Eternity' draws our attention toward an eternal perspective, inspiring us to live the present in the light of the glory to come.

About the impact of personal stories, Chapter 14: 'Unleashing the Power of Testimony' imparts the significance of sharing our experiences of grace and witnessing the profound effects these stories can have on the lives of others.

As we draw near to the session, the 'Concluding' section will recapitulate the key points discussed throughout the book and offer parting words of encouragement to embrace the Word as we progress in our spiritual voyage.

In the subsequent pages, your understanding may be expanded, your spirit uplifted, and your heart assured of the immutable truths that have anchored believers throughout the ages. Herein lies our structure, designed not as a rigid outline but as a map to be followed, leading us deeper into the heart and mind of God, enriching our faith, and revitalizing our practice. Let's embark upon this journey with anticipation for the insights to be gained and the transformations to be experienced.

Chapter 1:
The Foundation of Our Faith

In the soil of our souls, where belief takes root, the understanding of grace and the Word of God provide the essential nutrients for growth. Grace, as we'll see, is God's generous and unearned favor, reaching us in our darkest depths, with an origin that spans eternity and whispers into the fabric of all creation. It's where our faith begins and flourishes.

And as for the Word, it's not merely text on a page, but the living revelation of God, an anchor drawing us ever deeper into the unchanging truth of His promises. A steady light it serves to be, in the flurries and storms of existence, guiding our steps according to His unwavering purposes. Hence, in laying this groundwork, we embark on a lifelong journey to embrace a spiritual formation anchored firmly in these twin pillars: God's transforming grace and His illuminating Word.

Exploring the Biblical Concept of Grace

In continuing our journey into the foundation of our faith, we arrive at a cornerstone colossal in its implications yet intimate in its application: the biblical concept of grace. This is not simply a theological term to be mulled over by scholars but a profound reality that must be knit into the very fabric of our being. Grace, as presented in the Scriptures, emerges not as a reward for our achievements but as a generous outpouring of God's love, irrespective of our shortcomings.

To fully understand this truth, we must look into the original languages, where grace is known as "charis" in Greek, meaning favor, joy, and gratitude, and "chesed" in Hebrew, encapsulating loving-kindness and loyalty. This foundational understanding allows us to appreciate grace's role in our salvation and daily walk, revealing how it is both the starting block of our spiritual race and the tireless wind driving us forward.

As we delve deeper into the foundation of our faith, we come across a fundamental concept: the biblical concept of grace. This is not just a theological term to be studied by scholars but a profound reality that must be woven into the fabric of our being. Grace, as presented in the Scriptures, is not a reward for our achievements but a generous outpouring of God's love, regardless of our shortcomings.

Definition and Origins

The term 'grace' is rich with layers of meaning, each revealing a facet of the divine interaction with humanity. In its origins, 'grace' comes from the Greek word 'charis,' denoting favor, goodwill, and loving-kindness, especially when unmerited. This concept is not merely abstract but has been woven intricately into the faith narrative, starting from the earliest scriptural texts.

In the Old Testament, the Hebrew word often translated as 'grace' is 'Chen,' which also embodies the idea of favor, charm, and beauty, particularly the graciousness one finds in the eyes of another. It is most vividly illustrated in episodes where God provides protection, provision, and guidance without obligation but born out of His loving character.

The New Testament deepens this understanding by introducing 'grace' as an attribute of God and an active force in salvation and a sustaining presence in the believer's life. The coming of Jesus Christ embodies this grace, as the scriptures declare that grace and truth came into the world through Him.

As an origin point, grace is deeply rooted in the character of God, and the scriptures affirm that He is compassionate and gracious, slow to anger, and abounding in love. This sets the foundation for every expression of grace after that, which we understand not as something God does but as part of who He is. He is the wellspring from which all streams of grace flow.

The infusion of grace into human history began at creation when life itself was an act of divine grace, a testimony to God's generosity. As history unfolded, grace manifested itself in various covenants, highlighting a God that sustains a relationship with His creation despite its waywardness.

With the fall of man, grace took on the essential role of restoration, pointing us toward the redemptive work God had planned. In these early biblical stories, we find the seedlings of grace's promise, preparing the way for the full realization of grace in Christ Jesus.

Examples of grace abound from the patriarchs to the prophets. Noah found grace in the eyes of the Lord amidst a corrupt world. Abraham was also a recipient of God's grace, chosen to father a nation through which the world would be blessed. This theme of unmerited favor is a scarlet thread running through the tapestry of scripture.

The law, given through Moses, was another dimension of grace. It guided the people, set boundaries for living, and created a system for atonement that pointed toward the ultimate act of grace—the sacrifice of Christ. The law was a schoolmaster, leading us to Christ, where grace abounds even more.

In prophetic literature, we see grace promised, a future grace that would eclipse all former demonstrations as God's plan unfolded. This grace, spoken of in whispered tones throughout the ages, would one day be heralded at the birth of a child in a manger, the One who would be called 'the grace of God personified.'

The New Testament letters further expound on grace, teaching believers about the implications of grace for salvation and daily living. Here, grace is described as a gift, something one could never earn, providing the basis for justification and sanctification, where faith works through love.

Within early Christian communities, grace was understood as the active work of God through the Holy Spirit, enabling believers to live holy lives, giving them spiritual gifts for service, and binding them together in unity despite their diversity.

Paul, a critical figure in spreading the message of grace, often greeted and closed his letters with blessings of grace, underscoring its importance and ever-presence in the believer's life. His epistles delved into deep theological discussions on grace and provided practical instructions on how grace should permeate every aspect of Christian behavior.

Grace, as seen in the biblical narrative, is not static; it unfolds, reveals, and deepens over time. Its trajectory, beginning from the early whispers in Genesis and crescendo in the gospels, invites us to participate in this unfolding story of grace. It asks us to take up the mantle of grace, to live it, and to extend it to others.

In the very origins of grace, we find the threads that weave into the tapestry of the Christian vocation. Understanding grace shapes our identity, mission, and ultimate hope as people anchored in something greater than ourselves. The grace we find in scripture is an invitation to experience the very heart of the divine, leading us toward a life transformed and, in turn, transformative.

Thus, as we ponder the definition and origins of grace, we remember it is neither an abstract concept nor a mere theological construct. Grace is a reality to be lived and breathed, a dynamic presence, calling us to walk in the footsteps of the very grace that called the universe into being and calls each of us into a divine relationship marked by boundless love and mercy.

Understanding the Role of the Word in Our Lives

In the same way, a lamp casts light on a path and reveals the way forward; the Word of the Lord shines into our lives, offering guidance, wisdom, and a firm foundation upon which we can build. It's not just lines of text or a mere collection of historical events; it's a living, breathing source of life infused with the very essence of God's Spirit.

As we delve into the Scriptures, we find they are not a passive narrative but an active participant in our journey. They confront us in our complacency, challenge our misconceptions, and comfort us in our affliction. Through God's Word, we're equipped to navigate life's tumultuous seas, not merely by clinging to it as a life raft but by understanding its role as the very ship and compass – leading us to grace-filled horizons. Embracing the Word means letting it mold our hearts and minds, transforming our innermost beings, and aligning our desires with the purpose of God.

The Word as God's Revelation

At the heart of Christian belief is the profound truth that the Creator of the universe has not remained silent but has spoken to humanity. The means through which God has chosen to communicate is often referred to simply as the Word. It is an encompassing term intertwined with the very essence of God's act of revelation, bringing to light the character, will, and redeeming love of the divine.

The opening verses of the Gospel of John describe the Word as being with God in the beginning and being God. Thus, we gather that the Word is not merely a set of sounds or inscribed texts; it is life, light, and truth. Here, the Word is both cosmic and intimate, infusing creation with purpose and beckoning human hearts towards knowledge of the eternal.

The Scriptures stand as a testimony to God's relentless pursuit to make Himself known—a narrative unfolding from Genesis to Revelation. To apprehend the Word as God's revelation is to walk through a doorway that leads us to discover the very nature of God. His laws, His actions, His incarnation in Jesus Christ, all are facets of the Word that pull back the veil between humanity and the Divine.

In the storied history of Israel, the written Word—the Torah—served as an indelible link to the understanding of God's character. Through it, every teaching, commandment, or proverb offered a deeper insight into the righteousness, justice, and mercy central to God's nature. The psalmist writes, "Your word is a lamp for my feet, a light on my path," reflecting the Word's guiding role in turbulent times.

For believers, God's Word is not a relic of history; it remains vibrant and efficacious. The Epistle to the Hebrews describes it as living and active, sharper than any double-edged sword. In its pages, the divine and human meet, and the reader is not only informed but transformed—confronted with truths that penetrate the depths of the soul.

The prophets of old stood as bearers of God's Word, relaying divine messages that often cut against the grain of their culture. In a similar sense, the present-day faithful are called to grapple with the weighty implications of God's revealed Word. Proximity to the Word necessitates an awareness of the gravity of being God's image bearers and ambassadors.

In the economy of salvation, the Word has a pivotal purpose. It testifies to the culmination of God's plan—redemption through the life, death, and resurrection of Jesus Christ. The Gospels present Christ as the Word incarnate, the fullness of God's revelation embodied in human form, demonstrating the extent of divine love towards a fractured world.

Embracing the Word as God's revelation leads to a realization that it must permeate every aspect of our lives. It shapes perceptions, informs decisions, and governs actions. A life grounded in Scripture cannot help but look fundamentally different, as it is informed not by transient trends but by the timeless truths of God.

By understanding the Word as divine revelation, one can withstand the ebb and flow of society's changing morals and ethics. As we ingest and digest Scripture, it becomes part of our innermost being, refining and reshaping our character into the likeness of Christ. It is this Divine Word that instructs us in righteousness, reproof, correction, and training in righteousness, as stated by Paul to Timothy.

No serious consideration of the Word as divine revelation can ignore its communal aspect. Scripture, while deeply personal, is also a unifying thread that stitches believers together across cultural, linguistic, and denominational lines. It establishes a common narrative and shared language, forging bonds that transcend even the most profound earthly distinctions.

The transformative impact of the Word as God's revelation is evidenced not only in the inner workings of an individual's heart but also in the broader tapestry of society. Historically, movements undergirded by Scriptural principles have propelled societal advancement, championing causes such as justice, compassion, and dignity for all of humanity.

However, entry into the sacred texts requires humility—a humble recognition that God's ways and thoughts are higher than our own. It is through this humility that the Word is not only read or heard but received. This receptivity allows Scripture to nourish and sustain the spirit, just as Ezekiel ate the scroll, or Jeremiah found God's words and consumed them.

The process of engaging with the Word as divine revelation can be envisioned as a journey—one that begins with reverent listening and continues with diligent study, thoughtful meditation, and, most crucially, faithful application. It is through this continual engagement with Scripture that one's life becomes a living testament to God's transformative power.

Ultimately, the Word as God's revelation invites a response—a decision to live not according to one's own fleeting desires but in alignment with the divine purpose revealed in the text. Such a commitment requires perseverance, for the Word may challenge and convict as much as it comforts and assures.

In the quiet moments of reflection, as well as amid the clamor of daily life, the Word stands as a beacon of God's revelation. And so, embedded in the discipline of engaging with Scripture is the joyous discovery that God has indeed spoken, and His Word is a treasure trove of wisdom waiting to guide, to heal, and to draw souls into the sacred dance of redemption and life eternal.

The Word as Our Spiritual Anchor

In the tapestry of faith, threads of various hues and strengths are woven to create a picture of one's spiritual journey. Among these, none is so durable, so central to the fabric, as the Word of God. It is the firm foundation on which lives are built, the unwavering truth that guides believers through the shifting sands of circumstance. As we have seen in the previous sections, the Word is God's revelation, and now we consider its crucial role as our spiritual anchor.

Throughout history, the saints have relied on the scriptures to uphold them amid trials and triumphs alike. For the believer, the Word is not merely a collection of stories or wise sayings; it is the very lifeblood that sustains one's faith. Its verses are like the steady drumbeat to which the heart of the faithful syncs in times of both peace and peril.

It is written that "man shall not live by bread alone, but by every word that proceeds from the mouth of God" (Matthew 4:4). This profound truth speaks to the sustenance the scripture provides—a spiritual nourishment essential for growth and maturation. In this world brimming with fleeting delights and transient ideologies, the Word remains unchanged, a beacon of hope and wisdom for all generations.

The strength of the Word lies not in its historical context or poetic beauty, although it possesses both, but in its divine authorship. The breath of God imbued within each verse speaks directly to the individual soul, addressing needs and situations with uncanny precision. In the midst of life's storms, the Word is a steadfast presence, an anchor holding firm in spite of turbulent waves.

Brethren, consider how the Psalms have comforted the downcast, how the epistles have instructed the wayward, and how the Gospels have transformed the hardest of hearts. It is this living Word that equips us to face each day, not with anxious trepidation, but with unshakeable confidence.

Moreover, in the midst of confusion, the Word imparts wisdom, and in the scorching deserts of despair, it offers a wellspring of joy. The promises contained within its pages are not just for an age past but ring true for believers today. They are commitments from the Eternal One, assurances that He is indeed the same yesterday, today, and forever (Hebrews 13:8).

An intimate acquaintance with the Word is therefore indispensable. It is through the diligent study and heartfelt contemplation that one begins to discern the voice of the Shepherd amidst the clamor of many claimants. This practice fosters a spiritual acuity, allowing for the correction of one's path and alignment with divine will.

The experience of memorizing scripture and hiding it within one's heart creates an internal reservoir of truth that can be drawn upon in times of need. When temptation beckons or doubt looms, it is the memorized Word that rises within, fortifying the spirit and guiding actions.

It must not be forgotten, however, that the Word is not merely for the individual. It is also the glue that binds together the body of believers. In fellowship, the sharing and teaching of scripture contribute to collective edification, strengthening the church and empowering it to carry out its mission.

The practice of meditating on scripture is thus not a passive endeavor; it is the engagement of mind and heart with divine truth. As one chews on the Scriptures, turning over each phrase and pondering its meaning, transformation begins. It is a refining fire that shapes character, molds virtue, and instills wisdom.

Of course, challenges will arise. Distractions, doubts, and even the deceit of false teachings threaten to deviate the believer from the true course. But in these moments, it is the anchoring Word that provides the discernment needed to distinguish between truth and falsehood, between the fleeting fads of culture and the timeless truths of Christendom.

In cultivating a practice of daily devotions and scripture reading, one creates a rhythm of returning to the source of all hope. Each return not only serves to remind of God's faithfulness but also reinforces the anchor point in the soul.

There is a reciprocal relationship between the Word and prayer. As scripture informs and shapes one's supplications, so too do these conversations with the Almighty illuminate and deepen understanding of the scriptures. It is this synergy that empowers and emboldens the steps of faith.

In summary, the Word as our spiritual anchor is not simply a matter of intellectual assent or ritualistic reading. It is an ongoing relationship with the Holy Writ, a tapestry where the threads of personal experience, collective worship, and divine revelation are interwoven to create a resilient, sustaining, and life-giving connection with the Almighty.

Thus, brethren, let us hold fast to the anchor of the Word, that we may be steadfast and immovable, always abounding in the work of the Lord, knowing that in Him our labor is not in vain (1 Corinthians 15:58). Embrace the Word, for it is the wellspring of truth, the light on our path, and the very power of God unto salvation for everyone who believes (Romans 1:16).

Chapter 2:
Grace as a Divine Sponsor

In the grand narrative of faith, grace emerges as a Divine Sponsor, initiating our journey towards spiritual rebirth and sustaining us throughout life's tumultuous seas. This unmerited favor, lavishly bestowed upon us, becomes the cornerstone upon which our relationship with the Creator stands. It's in this unearned sponsorship where our souls find rest and our spirits are enlivened.

As we delve deeper into grace's transformative power, we'll uncover the layers of its profound influence on our lives—how it reshapes the human heart and redirects our path towards a divinity-kissed destiny. Grace does not merely accompany faith; it ignites it, nurturing a symbiotic dance where faith blossoms in response to the Divine's generous overture. Within grace's embrace, believers discover their true strength, recognizing that in their inherent weakness, the magnificence of God's sponsorship shines brightest, inviting a life lived not by sight but by the sure certainty of faith—an assurance wrapped in the eternal kindness of the One who calls the stars by name and holds our lives in His hands.

Grace as God's Unmerited Favor

In the landscape of divine truths, grace stands as a beacon of God's generous heart, illuminating the path for the weary and the burdened. This grace, inherently a manifestation of God's unmerited favor, is freely bestowed upon us, not because of what we've accomplished but because of His overflowing love and mercy.

It's like the sun's warming rays touching the earth without requiring it to merit such radiance. Grace cannot be earned by deeds or human effort; it flows from the divine wellspring, seeking those hollow from their toils and troubles. When grace descends upon life, it is both a salve and a catalyst – soothing the soul's wounds with its comforting presence and igniting a transformation from within. This alchemy turns the dross of our humanity into the gold of godly purpose. This grace is at the heart of our relationship with the Creator, a relentless current that carries us forward, even when we falter and fall.

How Grace Transforms Our Lives

Understanding the transformative power of grace is essential in a believer's journey. The infusion of grace into one's life can be subtle and revolutionary, reshaping dreams, desires, and deeds in ways that align more closely with God's heart. Grace acts not merely as a pardon for past wrongs but as a catalyst for personal reformation. In the boundless expanses of grace, individuals find the power to overcome habitual failings, the wisdom to discern right from wrong, and the courage to walk in righteousness.

Grace enters into the crevices of our brokenness with tender mercy. When life casts a shadow upon us, when despair grips our soul, grace whispers words of comfort and infuses strength into our weary bones. For grace speaks of God's commitment to us, unswerving and unwavering, despite the fragility of our human condition. It reassures us that we are eternally anchored to something—or Someone—far greater than the turbulence of our immediate circumstances.

In the context of our past, grace offers redemption, ensuring that our mistakes do not define us. It allows us to look back, not with a heart mired in regret, but with one that recognizes growth. Grace teaches that each misstep is an opportunity for learning and that each failure is a steppingstone to wisdom. This liberating understanding propels us forward, unshackled by the chains of former transgressions.

Grace also shapes our interactions, coloring how we perceive others and ourselves. It encourages patience and empathy, urging us to extend kindness where judgment might instead prevail. When faced with a friend's shortcomings or the waywardness of a loved one, grace equips us to respond with a love that reflects the heartbeat of the divine.

Amid our daily existence, grace acts as an ever-present teacher, instructing us in gratitude. Gratitude rooted in grace acknowledges the value of the present moment, the gifts woven into the ordinary, and the rich tapestry of blessings that might otherwise go unnoticed. Grace opens our eyes to the beauty surrounding us and tunes our hearts to the sublime symphony of life.

When envisioning our future, grace provides a lens of hope. It assures us that our destinies are not left to chance but are sculpted by a loving Creator who weaves purpose into every thread of our story. With this assurance, we can approach our tomorrows with serene confidence, knowing that the narrative of our lives is in the hands of a masterful Author.

In the sphere of our calling and vocation, grace imparts significance. It illuminates our talents, dreams, and passions, encouraging us to pursue a purpose that transcends mere personal gain. We find ourselves caught up in a larger narrative that involves blessing others, fostering community, and healing the broken parts of this world.

On the battleground of temptation, grace offers us victory. It empowers us not by relying on our frail willpower but by surrendering to a strength that is not our own. Grace is our fortification against the forces that seek to lead us astray, equipping us with the armor of divine righteousness and the sword of spiritual fortitude.

Within the context of our limitations, grace teaches humility. It reminds us that we are not the heroes of our own story but rather participants in the unfolding drama of redemption authored by God. This humility does not lead to self-abasement but to a freeing acceptance of our dependence on a power greater than ourselves.

For those who labor under the weight of guilt, grace is unburdening. No longer must one remain shackled to the prison of self-condemnation; grace declares liberty and proclaims a new identity. This new identity is not marred by sin but instead marked by a redeemed nature, signifying our adoption as children of the Most High.

In the face of adversity, grace provides resilience. When suffering looms large and mists of doubt obscure the path ahead, grace lights the way, ensuring that even our darkest nights are illuminated by the divine presence's faint but certain glow. This resilience carries us through tribulations, transforming trials into testimonies of perseverance and strength.

Transpiration of holiness arises as grace does its sanctifying work within us. Once tainted by self-interest, our actions become offerings of love, sacrificial and pure. Daily, the believer is called to a pursuit of holiness, buttressed by grace, realizing that it is not a result of moral striving but a surrender to the ongoing work of God within the eager heart.

Grace instills a spirit of generosity. One touched by grace becomes a conduit through which love and compassion flow to others. Moved by the profound gift of grace received, we are propelled to give freely, serve joyfully, and touch lives with the same grace that has radically altered our own.

In cultivating relationships, grace is the wellspring from which forgiveness flows. The knowledge of having been forgiven much fosters within us a capability to forgive others. Holding onto grievances is replaced by release, bitterness by blessing, strife by peace—all outcomes of the transformative work of grace.

Finally, grace is our anchor in the journey toward our eternal horizon. It assures us that this world is a foretaste of the glory that awaits. With our eyes fixed on eternity, grace shapes our perspective, enabling us to live vigorously in the present while longing for the ultimate fulfillment of God's gracious promise—the restoration of all things and the everlasting joy found in His presence.

Examples of Grace in the Bible

As we reflect on the transformative power of grace, it's invaluable to turn to the scriptures to witness firsthand how grace has worked throughout history. Within the Bible, countless narratives unfold showcasing God's unmerited favor. One such poignant example is the life of Noah. In Genesis, it is said that Noah found grace in the eyes of the Lord (Genesis 6:8). Amidst a world ensnared by corruption, Noah stood as a beacon of righteousness—not by his merit, but by the grace bestowed upon him.

Consider too the story of Abraham, called out of his country to a land he did not know. Abraham's journey exemplifies the grace of calling and election. God's promise to Abraham in Genesis 12 was not based upon his deeds but upon God's good pleasure and sovereign choice. Through grace, Abraham becomes the father of many nations, an heir of the world—not through the law, but through the righteousness of faith.

Joseph's life in Egypt reflects grace in the face of injustice and suffering. Betrayed by his brothers and wrongfully imprisoned, Joseph could have descended into bitterness. Yet, the grace of God was with him, causing him to rise to a position where he could not only save Egypt but also his family, which had wronged him. The grace seen in Joseph's story is multifaceted—redemption, provision, and reconciliation all intertwine.

The exodus of the Israelites from Egypt showcases God's grace in deliverance. God's people were not liberated because of their righteousness, but by grace, they were chosen to be His people. In Deuteronomy 7:7-8, it is clear: it was not because of their size or might but because the Lord loved them and kept the oath He swore to their ancestors.

The narrative of Ruth introduces us to a Moabite woman who found favor, or grace, in the eyes of Boaz, a reflection of God's grace towards those outside of Israel. Ruth's story is a testament to how grace breaks barriers and unites disparate lives within the grand tapestry of redemption's story.

David's anointing as king, despite his humble beginnings and subsequent sin with Bathsheba, tells of grace that anoints and redeems. Even his penitential psalms, especially Psalm 51, echo with cries for grace's restoring touch upon a contrite heart. God's covenant with David, extending to his descendants forever, exemplifies grace in promise and kingship.

Fast-forwarding to the New Testament, one cannot discuss grace without centering on the life and ministry of Jesus Christ. In John 1:14-17, the Word becoming flesh is described as full of grace and truth, and from this fullness, we have all received grace upon grace. Christ's parables, healing, and ultimate sacrifice illuminate the breadth and depth of God's grace.

The parable of the prodigal son (Luke 15:11-32) vividly paints a picture of grace that awaits with open arms. The wayward son, expecting judgment, is met instead with a father's embrace—an image of Divine Grace greeting us upon our return from wanderings.

Paul's dramatic conversion on the road to Damascus is yet another robust illustration of grace. A persecutor of Christians, Paul encounters Christ and is transformed into a foremost apostle—demonstrating that grace can redirect the most unlikely lives towards God's purposes.

Similarly, the story of Peter illustrates grace in restoration. After denying Christ thrice, Peter is not cast aside. Instead, he is tenderly restored by Jesus after the resurrection and becomes a pivotal figure in the early Church. Peter's life serves as a testimony that grace is stronger than our failures.

One of the most eloquent discourses on grace can be found in Ephesians 2:8-9, where Paul asserts that it is by grace that we are saved, through faith—and this is not from ourselves, it is the gift of God. This tenet encapsulates grace as foundational to salvation—it cannot be earned, only received.

In 2 Corinthians 12:7-10, Paul speaks of a "thorn in the flesh" and the repeated plea for its removal. The Lord's response, "My grace is sufficient for you, for my power is made perfect in weakness," affirms grace as sustaining in times of trial and weakness, underscoring grace as strength when we are most vulnerable.

The Book of Hebrews, chapters 4 and 11, further highlights grace in the context of rest and faith. We encounter a God who provides a rest—a grace-imbued promise of peace and cessation from labors—and a hall of faith where men and women from diverse backgrounds obtain a good report through faith, underpinned by grace.

Last, we are brought face to face with grace as a future hope in Revelation. The promise of a new heaven and new earth, the grace-filled invitation that "whosoever will" may come and partake of the water of life freely, speaks to a culminating grace that stretches into eternity.

Each of these biblical episodes invites contemplation on the variegated nature of grace—calling, redeeming, sustaining, and consummating. As we immerse ourselves in these accounts, let us remember that the same grace active in the lives of these individuals is available to transform, sustain, and guide us today.

The Symbiotic Relationship Between Grace and Faith

In the journey through the landscape of divine grace, we find its terrain inextricably intertwined with the essence of faith. Grace, described as God's unmerited favor, exists not as a remote concept but as an engaging invitation to trust, which faith eagerly accepts and reciprocates.

As a divine sponsor, grace initiates the relationship, offers life beyond our frailties and shortcomings, and faith—our heartfelt response—embraces this gift, growing deeper into the soul-humbling truth of God's boundless love. This union of grace and faith is neither fleeting nor superficial; the profound symbiosis nourishes the believer's spirit.

Faith is the breath that animates grace's body; it becomes the inherent action prompted by the realization of a life unearned yet generously given. Through this sacred dance of reciprocity, one witness the miraculous unfolding of a life transformed—a testament to the power dwelling within the harmonious embrace of grace and faith.

Faith's Response to Grace

In the heartfelt exploration of grace and its profound impact on our lives, it's essential to recognize the manner in which faith serves as the heartfelt response to this divine benevolence. Faith can be likened to the bloom that follows the downpour of grace—it is an organic, burgeoning realization that we are deeply loved and mercifully provided for by our Creator.

When grace descends unearned and liberally upon a person, it serves not as a conclusion to spiritual development but as a vital commencement. It is faith, that deeply personal yet universally accessible quality, which receiveth this grace, affirming its truth and incorporating it into the fabric of one's life. This faith stirreth within the soul, a profound recognition of grace's transformative power that cannot help but elicit a joyful and determined response.

Faith, authentic in its essence, does not remain a static testament; it rises up in action. It's through faith that a person begins to shift from being a passive recipient of grace to an active participant in God's plan. The life awash with grace is thereby marked by an enduring trust in the purposes of the Lord, even when they lie beyond the horizon of human understanding.

This trust, inherently bound to the concept of faith, finds itself tested in the tempests of life. Yet, it is precisely in the midst of stormy trials that faith's response to grace shows its true mettle. The believer, steadied by the unshakeable knowledge of God's goodness, can stand firm, knowing that grace is both the anchor amidst turbulence and the compass towards serenity.

As such, faith does not merely accept grace; it also emulates it. The faith-filled life increasingly mirrors the generosity of the Lord it so fervently believes in. One might discover themselves extending forgiveness without dispute, offering love without condition, and serving others without expectation of recognition or repayment.

The scriptures intimate that faith and works are inextricably linked, asserting that faith without works is devoid of life. This does not undermine the principle that salvation is by grace alone, but it does highlight the inexorable truth that genuine faith is dynamic and expressive. The faith that responds to grace consequently moves one toward deeds that reflect the kingdom's values, drawing them ever closer to the heart of the Father.

Moreover, faith grows in proportion to the measure in which it is exercised. As grace is more deeply understood and valued, faith expands, augmenting the believer's capacity to receive and share grace further. The journey of faith is, in essence, a progressive discovery and re-discovery of God's munificent grace.

This relationship between faith and grace is symbiotic—each springs from and nourishes the other. Faith is the soul's confidence in the veracity of grace promised, and as such, becomes the means by which grace is operationalized in the believer's life. The gifts of grace—in forgiveness, redemption, and provision—are realized and made effective through faith.

The aforementioned gifts, once entrenched in the life of faith, cannot help but radiate outward. The love and mercy that one experiences through grace naturally engenders a desire to share this treasure with others. Faith understands that grace is not a commodity meant for hoarding, but a boundless resource intended for dispersal.

It is in this space of sharing and community where faith's response to grace is most vibrant and visible. There exists a kindred spirit among believers, united by the shared experience of God's grace, which engenders a unique fellowship. Within this fellowship, faith finds expression in encouragement, support, and sometimes even gentle correction, all underscored by the unchanging truth of grace.

Furthermore, faith doesn't only look to the 'now' but also gazes firmly to the hope of what lies beyond. The grace that has been so abundantly showered in this life is but a foretaste of the glory that awaits. Therefore, faith abides with a gaze affixed on eternity, living out grace with the knowledge that the fullness of its beauty and completeness is, as yet unseen.

In practice, this faith—which is a response to grace—is nurtured through regular communion with the divine, primarily through His Word and prayer. These disciplines, engaged in with a spirit of expectancy and reverence, ensure that the response to grace is both rooted and flourishing. Faith relies not on fleeting feelings but on the steadfast and trustworthy nature of God as revealed in His promises.

Yet, the beauty of faith's response to grace is that it is not a one-size-fits-all formula. Each believer, in the uniqueness of their journey, encounters and responds to grace in manifold ways—though all are anchored in the same ultimate truths. This diversity within unity not only enhances the body of Christ, but it also serves as a testament to the boundless creativity of the God of grace.

In closing, faith's response to grace is pivotal in crafting a life that resonates with the very heartbeat of the Gospel. It is an ever-evolving, deeply personal, and beautifully communal experience. It stands as an act of worship, a declaration of trust, and an outpouring of love, forever testifying to the boundless grace of God which first called it forth.

For those traversing the path of faith, the response to grace finds its ultimate expression in a life lived out loud for the glory of God—manifest in love, rooted in truth, and brimming with the undying hope of the Gospel. The journey of faith, then, is the glorious adventure of learning, heartbeat by heartbeat, the unfathomable depths of grace—and responding with a life that sings its praise.

Living by Faith

As we turn from a focus on the transformative power of Grace to the practical outworking of Faith in one's life, the concept of living by Faith becomes crucial. This is not a transient step in the spiritual journey but rather a steadfast walk, a fundamental lifestyle emulating the righteousness of the Biblical patriarchs who "by faith" obtained a good testimony (Hebrews 11). Living by Faith is the response of the human soul to the divine echo of God's unwavering promise; it's laying hold of the invisible while navigating the tangible.

The Bible says, "The Just shall live by faith" (see Habakkuk 2:4). It is to be believed that Faith sustains life. Yet Faith is not common in man because his soul is puffed up even though it is not upright within him. If the righteous shall live by his Faith, the adjourning question is by whose righteousness, if not Christ Jesus? God is the ultimate source and reason of Faith; otherwise, what we know as humans merely expresses speculations based on what aligns with our sensory expectations.

Consider for a moment the lilies of the field as depicted in Matthew 6:28-30. They toil not, neither do they spin, yet Solomon in all his glory was not arrayed like one of these. Here, we find a principle of Faith: complete reliance on the Creator's provision. Faith exudes silent confidence, a serene trust that does not fret in the face of scarcity, but rests assured in the Lord's fidelity.

It must be understood that Faith is not passive; it's active. James 2:17 reminds us that Faith without works is dead. Active Faith is Abraham stepping out into an unknown land, Noah building an ark for rain he had never seen, and Rahab harboring spies for a future she could not fully grasp. Our actions rooted in Faith will not always conform to the logic of this world, for they are conceived in the realm where God's voice directs, and His assurance suffices.

One's journey in Faith is not void of challenge. It is these very trials that refine and define a living trust. As gold is tested by fire, so our Faith, much more precious than perishable gold, may be tried with fire to result in praise, glory, and honor at the revelation of Jesus Christ (1 Peter 1:7). Trials mold Faith into an unshakable foundation that withstands the weathers of life.

To live by Faith is to abide in hope, a hope that serves as an anchor of the soul, both sure and steadfast (Hebrews 6:19). Amid the stormy seas of life, this anchor holds not because of the strength of the vessel but because of the reliability of the ground it grasps—Christ Himself. This hope never disappoints because God's love has been poured into our hearts (Romans 5:5).

Faith, though personal, is not meant to be an isolated endeavor. The Body of Christ is a tapestry of faith stories woven together, each narrative bringing encouragement and fortitude to one another (Hebrews 10:24-25). Our testimonies inspire Faith in others, and we find a multiplicative effect of strengthened resolve and mutual edification in communal sharing.

In the sphere of living by Faith, prayer stands as a vital conduit. It opens the heavens, aligning our minds with divine perspectives and bringing power to our earthly petitions (Philippians 4:6). Through prayer, we relinquish our illusion of control and firmly grasp the hem of His providential governance.

To walk by Faith is to be directed by a vision beyond the visible. It is to envision a day when every tear will be wiped away, and Faith shall be made sight (Revelation 21:4). Focus on this eternal horizon drives one's daily prioritization and decision-making, cultivating a life of spiritual substance and eternal consequence.

Indeed, living by Faith necessitates a posture of surrender. This surrender is not a defeat but rather a triumphant entry into the freedom that comes from God's will being our command. We are slaves to righteousness, instruments of God's peace. As we yield ourselves, we "put on the Lord Jesus Christ" (Romans 13:14), and we will harmoniously align with His.

The Scriptures brim with exhortation to walk by Faith and not by sight (2 Corinthians 5:7). This walk is not charted by worldly wisdom or sightlines but advances step by step in sync with the Holy Spirit's rhythm. It is a journey staked on promises of "Yes and Amen" in Christ (2 Corinthians 1:20), entrenched in acknowledging God's overarching sovereignty.

Living by Faith is an invaluable witness to a watching world. As a tree is known by its fruit, so is living faith known by the visible outworking of an internal conviction. Our lives become an open letter, read by all, a testimony to the Grace of God and the truth He has bestowed upon us through His Word.

Moreover, Faith is not merely for one's advancement but is to be shared. To hold belief in one's heart and not extend it to a neighbor is counterintuitive to the gospel call. An active faith beckons the believer to reach out, serve, love, and speak words of life in a backdrop often devoid of hope.

The vitality of Faith in the journey of a believer's life cannot be overstated. We were saved through Faith, are being sanctified through Faith, and will one day see the fullness of our salvation because of religion. It is the bedrock upon which the message of Grace and truth stands resolute, the fertile soil where seeds of hope are planted and harvested for glory.

As we journey forward, let the light of Faith not flicker but burn steadfastly, guiding us through valleys and over mountains. Through every season, let Faith be our constant companion, a guiding star, and a firm foundation. For whatever is born of God overcomes the world. And this victory has overcome the world—our Faith (1 John 5:4).

Living by Faith is a call to spiritual adventure, a divine summons to trust profoundly in the One who is faithful. Journey on, then, with resilience and joy, for the path of Faith is the path of life, and on it lies the treasures of Heaven promised to those who persevere. May these truths guide us as we explore the nuances and the practicalities of such a devoted faith walk with the Lord.

Chapter 3:
Anchored in the Word

Emerging from a comprehensive exploration of grace's profound dimensions, we now pivot to the quintessence of Christian certitude: the luminous beacon of Scripture. In the labyrinth of life's tempests, the Bible serves not as a mere guidepost but as our undying, steadfast spiritual compass. It is here, within its infallible and sufficient teachings, that one's soul can tether securely, resisting the gales of uncertainty and doubt.

It's imperative we nurture a deep and abiding connection to the Word, for in its layers and verses lies the framework of a resolute faith. As we delve into the process of absorbing Scripture, embracing its truths, we simultaneously enkindle the flame of our spiritual yearnings. It is an endeavor that demands diligence, yet promises immeasurable reward, as the sanctity of divine instruction molds our discernment and guides our footsteps. In embracing the sacred text, one finds the wellspring of wisdom to navigate the complexities of existence with grace-filled confidence.

The Bible as Our Spiritual Compass

Nothing is more critical than a compass in the mariner's life, unwaveringly guiding them through the treacherous and unpredictable seas. Similarly, for us, as believers navigating the profound depths of existence, the Bible serves as our spiritual compass, offering unwavering direction amidst life's tumultuous waves.

As our journey from the foundational understanding of grace unfolds, we draw upon the Scriptures, acknowledging their divine inspiration and enduring authority. These sacred texts stand infallible, shepherding us through life's bewildering array of choices and challenges, steering us not by the shifting sands of cultural conviction but by the bedrock truths of God's eternal wisdom.

Each verse, chapter, and book within the Holy Writ forms a mosaic of guidance, illuminating the path for a life imprinted with the Lord's grace and anchored in righteous living. And as we earnestly consult this celestial chart, we cultivate a sensitivity to the Spirit's whisper, discovering the invigorating power to live out our faith with confidence and genuine transformation.

The Infallibility of Scripture

In the journey through the rich landscape of faith, we have come to understand the transformative power of grace which is splendidly woven into the fabric of our lives. Now, we set our sights on a cornerstone of our belief as we delve into the infallibility of Scripture. The Scriptures stand resolute, a beacon that has guided countless souls through the tumults of life and promise to be the unshakable foundation upon which we can build our understanding and growth.

The divine inspiration of the Holy Scriptures declares them to be without error in their original writings. They hold up under the scrutiny of earnest seekers, offering timeless truths that are applicable to every facet of life. This infallibility means that the Bible, in its entirety, is dependable, trustworthy, and incapable of leading us astray when interpreted correctly.

Let us contemplate the prophetic works that, spanning centuries, have not faltered or contradicted themselves. Such precision and consistency across diverse authors, contexts, and eras speak to a divine choreography that anchors these writings beyond the capabilities of mere human contrivance.

Our faith is thereby grounded in a text that withstands the weathering of time and culture. The promises enclosed within its pages have been tested and found steadfast. Believers can wholeheartedly entrust themselves to the guidance it provides, for it is the embodiment of truth revealed by a God who embodies truth itself.

Some may raise questions or cast doubts on certain passages, yet these instances often stem from a limited perspective or a misinterpretation of the text. The infallibility of Scripture does not imply that readers will always understand it completely; rather, it assures us that the Scripture, in its essence and intent, is entirely reliable.

A profound comfort can be drawn from the realization that these sacred words are not subject to the changing tides of human opinion. Values and philosophies may evolve, but the Word of God remains fixed, a testament to its divine origin and an unchanging God.

It is crucial, then, to approach Scripture with reverence and humility, recognizing our own limitations and seeking the guidance of the Holy Spirit for interpretation. In doing so, we submit to the will and wisdom of God, allowing the true meaning and application of His Word to be revealed in our lives.

Through the infallibility of Scripture, we are equipped with a moral compass that points unwaveringly toward righteousness. The ethical dilemmas and choices we face are met with clear direction from the Word of God, which speaks with authority on matters of conduct and character.

Moreover, the infallible Word serves as an anchor for our doctrines. Rather than being tossed about by the waves of novel teachings or seductive heresies, we can cling to the biblical tenets that have sustained the faithful throughout the ages.

With the Scriptures as our firm foundation, we can confidently address life's most searching questions and profound longings. Our quest for meaning, purpose, and hope is met within the hallowed verses that proclaim a narrative larger than ourselves—a redemptive story that encompasses all of creation.

Even as the infallible Scriptures confront us with the reality of our human condition, they also elevate us to our true identity in Christ. They eschew the flattery of human ego and yet offer the healing balm of grace that remakes and redeems us.

The narratives, laws, poetry, and prophecies contained within the Bible form a cohesive and comprehensive guide for living. The flawless harmony of its content undergirds every aspect of our daily practice, providing wisdom for interaction and insight for internal reflection.

In a world clouded by uncertainty and shadowed by misinformation, the infallible nature of Scripture emerges as a beacon of absolute truth. It calls us out of confusion into the clarity provided by God's revealed Word, enduring as an unshakeable testament to the Almighty's sovereignty and love.

For believers, the infallible Word manifests as a source of hope and strength. It provides solace during trials, as the heroic accounts of faith, the psalms of lamentation and praise, and the prophetic assurances of deliverance all testify to a God who is intimately acquainted with our suffering and ardently devoted to our flourishing.

Embracing the infallibility of Scripture is to embrace a journey of discovery, where each verse has the potential to become a stepping stone to deeper faith. It's where the historical becomes personal, the heavenly touches the earthly, and the words of God speak directly into the heart of the believer.

As we behold the unfailing Word, we are invited into a relationship with the Author Himself – an invitation that both challenges us and cherishes us, and ultimately transforms us. The infallible Scriptures ask us to not only believe in their content but also to act upon it, allowing its truths to become the very fabric of our lives, shaping us into the likeness of Christ, the Living Word.

In the fabric of faith, we thread the warp on the loom of our lives with the very fiber of the Word. **The Sufficiency of Scripture** is a majestic mountain peak within the landscape of divine revelation, standing sentinel to the reality that in God's Word, we have all that is necessary for life and godliness. It's in the divine breath of Scripture that we discover the sublime meaning of sufficiency. For within its lines and between its verses lies the roadmap to navigating the thoroughfares of our existence.

The concept of Scripture's sufficiency is transformative: it assures us that the Bible is completely adequate to instruct us in every aspect of faith and practice. It is this very sufficiency which provides every man and woman with the tools needed for the journey of life, encompassing all there is to know for leading a life pleasing to God. It is the cornerstone of our faith, asserting that the Scripture requires no addition, no contemporary update, no supplement to fulfill its divine role.

God, in His gracious providence, did not merely inspire the writers of the Bible; He protected their words through centuries – that they might be a wellspring of wisdom for all generations. This provision is testimony to the enduring power of Scripture, its capacity to speak into the lives of people across time and culture. As our world changes and challenges multiply, the Word stands immutable, unerringly true, and invariably relevant.

We must recognize that the advocacy for the sufficiency of Scripture is not ignorance of the complexities and nuances of human experience. Rather, it is the acknowledgment that the Scriptures hold timeless principles that apply to the very intricacies of our contemporary lives. It acts as the lens through which we should view every situation, be it trials, relationships, ethical dilemmas, or spiritual warfare.

The wonderful assurance that Scripture is sufficient fortifies the believer's heart to resist the temptation to seek answers outside the divine narrative. It propels a confidence that the Holy Book is not merely an ancient manuscript but the living, active word of God, discerning our thoughts and attitudes, fitting, and refitting us for every good work.

Indubitably, the Bible's sufficiency does not eliminate the need for diligent study and the application of its truth. To plumb the depths of Scripture requires an ongoing commitment to reading, meditation, and prayer. God's truth is revealed progressively to those who seek Him earnestly, and the Spirit enlightens the mind to understand the treasures contained within.

Embracing the Bible's sufficiency shapes our approach to personal growth and sanctification. It does not advocate a quietist approach to spirituality, whereby one is passive. It calls the believer to active engagement with Scripture, discerning the heartbeat of God, and aligning one's life with His eternal will.

There can be no greater joy for the believer than discovering that God has provided all that is needed for life's journey in His Word. A life anchored in this truth is like a ship securely moored, able to withstand the fiercest of storms. It is the knowledge of the Scripture's sufficiency that equips believers in their darkest hour, offering solace and strength that is not of this world.

The sufficiency of Scripture also provides an anchor in the shifting sands of cultural relativism. It affirms that truth is neither antiquated nor variable but enduring and absolute, resting upon the sure foundation laid down by the Creator Himself. This confidence permits the building of lives that reflect the character of Christ, immutable against the tides of change.

Furthermore, the sufficiency of Scripture compels us to a greater accountability. For if in the Bible we possess all that is necessary for instruction in righteousness, then it is to these holy texts we must look for guidance. It behooves us to study, to understand, and to apply the divine precepts with rigor and reverence, shaping our lives after the pattern presented therein.

When we commit ourselves to the sufficient Word, we shall find that not only is our understanding heightened, but so too is our ability to navigate the complexities of human relationships and the demands of everyday living. We're given a vocabulary of grace, forgiveness, compassion, and courage, all drawn from the well of Scripture.

Lastly, drawing upon the sufficiency of Scripture leads us to respond with a heart of gratitude. We are recipients of a grace so profound; it has provided everything essential for communion with the father. This gratitude translates into a life of worship, demonstrated in obedience, service, and a burning desire to share the treasure we have in the Word.

The doctrine of the sufficiency of Scripture is not a dry theological tenet to be relegated to dusty shelves of academic debate. It is a wellspring of eternal truth, a fountain of divine wisdom, and a guiding beacon in the often-turbulent sea of human experience. As we journey through each chapter of life, may the sufficiency of Scripture serve as our compass and comfort, our guide and guardian, revealing the fullness of God's grace for every step of the way.

Nurturing a Deep Connection with the Word

Fostering a relationship with God's Word isn't merely an intellectual exercise; it's a practice that can fill the soul with unfathomable richness. To nurture this profound connection, one might begin by setting aside dedicated time for reading and reflection, ensuring Scripture becomes an integral part of daily rhythms. It's about immersing oneself in the biblical narrative, allowing the truths to seep into every crevice of life. As one delves into the Scripture, it's crucial to approach it with a teachable spirit, seeking understanding through prayer and meditation.

By memorizing verses, God's promises and commandments become an internal compass, guiding actions and decisions. Yet, embracing the Word isn't an endeavor one undertakes in isolation; it's enriched by sharing insights with fellow believers, discussing passages, and encouraging one another in the truth. Over time, perseverance in these disciplines matures a seedling faith into a sturdy tree deeply rooted in the fertile soil of sacred Scripture.

Practical Steps for Studying Scripture

Embarking on a journey through Scripture is likened to navigating a vast and splendid terrain rich with history, mystery, and divine instruction. It's essential to approach this exploration with reverence and a systematic plan to gain depth of understanding and practical application. Here, we will outline practical steps that facilitate an enriching study of the Bible.

First and foremost, designate a specific time and place for your study. Consistency is critical to building a habit and ensuring that your engagement with the Word becomes part of your daily rhythm. Whether at dawn's early light or in the evening's tranquil moments, find a time that allows you to be alert and free from distractions.

Equip yourself with the right tools. A trustworthy Bible translation, a notebook, and pens for journaling your insights are fundamental. Additionally, having a solid Bible commentary and access to lexicons for original language study can enrich your understanding, though they aren't strictly necessary for everyone.

Begin your study with prayer. As you enter Scripture, invite the Holy Spirit (the Author) to illuminate the text, speak to your heart, and guide your understanding. You recognize that the Word is living and active, inviting an engagement beyond mere intellectual pursuit and into relational depth.

Choose a book of the Bible to study. Decide on a starting point if you feel drawn to poetic writings, historical accounts, or epistles. You might start with one of the Gospels, which provides the foundation of the Christian faith, abounding in grace and truth.

Situate the text within its proper context. Understanding the Author, audience, cultural backdrop, and purpose of the writing is vital. This step prevents misinterpretation and helps apply the Scripture appropriately to your life.

Employ a study method, such as the inductive method, which involves observation, interpretation, and application. This process allows you to extract meaning from the text and consider how it changes you and your life.

Engage with the Scripture slowly and thoughtfully. Read and then reread passages, chewing on the words and pondering their meaning. Consider reading out loud to engage more of your senses, aiding memory and comprehension.

Document your discoveries and questions in a journal. Writing things down helps retention and creates a personal record of your spiritual journey through the scriptures.

Focus on memorization. Committing Scripture to memory means you carry the power of God's Word wherever you go, allowing it to shape your thoughts and actions continually.

Contemplate and meditate on the passages. Christian meditation involves filling your mind with Scripture, mulling it over, and letting it dwell richly within you. This is the bedrock of transformation, allowing the words to become ingrained in your soul.

Application is the fruit of study. Ask yourself how the Scripture relates to your life, what it calls you to change, and how it guides your decisions. Be specific in identifying actionable steps in your daily walk.

Additionally, engage in community-based study. Share your insights and questions with a group or a friend. This communal aspect enriches the study as different perspectives emerge and mutual encouragement abounds. It is within the context of 'iron sharpening iron' that deeper truths are often discovered.

When encountering confusing or challenging texts, don't shy away. Instead, seek resources, seek wisdom from a more seasoned believer, or delve into further study. Perseverance in study often leads to profound moments of revelation and understanding.

Finally, let your study of scripture spill over into worship. As you grow in your understanding of God's Word, let it lead you to moments of awe, praise, and a more profound sense of God's vast grace in your life. Scripture is not only for knowledge but is a pathway to encountering the divine and standing in wonder of the grand narrative of redemption we are invited into.

These steps, anchored in a humble and earnest pursuit of truth, are tools to build a robust and vibrant understanding of Scripture. As one integrates these practices, the Bible becomes more than a book; it becomes nourishment, a living wellspring of wisdom, and the very light for our path.

Overcoming Common Challenges

Every pilgrim journeying along the path of faith confronts a myriad of challenges. One formidable undertaking is nurturing a deep connection with the Word of God. As believers anchor themselves in Scripture, they may face trials akin to headwinds, striving to topple their resolve and hinder their progress. In this treatise, efforts shall be focused on surmounting those common obstacles that believers might face while engaging with the Holy Scriptures.

It is expected to find oneself besieged by distractions, as secular and sacred, mundane and momentous, vie for attention. In this digital age, the siren call of devices may lead even the most well-intentioned astray from daily communion with God's Word. To overcome this, one must intentionally carve out designated times for Scripture, fashioning a sanctuary of silence where the soul might meet with the Divine without interruption.

Another challenge frequently encountered is the perception of Scripture as antiquated or irrelevant. In grappling with this, it is essential to pray for insight and approach the Word with expectancy, trusting that the Spirit who inspired its authors is the identical alive within us today, eager to illuminate its truths for our lives and times.

The sheer complexity and depth of the Bible can also prove daunting. Therefore, wisdom seekers are well-counseled to embark with patience, allowing layers of understanding to unveil themselves progressively. Supplementing personal reading with communal study can provide a richness of perspective and mutual encouragement in the quest for comprehension.

Moreover, feelings of inadequacy may assail believers, whispering that one's grasp of theology or Scripture is insufficient. These murmurs must be met with the assurance that every disciple is a lifelong learner and that the grasp one has today is the foundation upon which tomorrow's understanding will be built.

For some, the challenge lies in applying scriptural teachings to the complexities of modern existence. Such an endeavor requires prayer, reflection, and counsel from fellow believers, ensuring that scriptural truths are not merely admired but lived.

Doubt, a subtler adversary, can creep into the heart, questioning the integrity or divine origin of Scripture. Against this, one must wield the shield of faith, trusting in the testimony of countless saints who, across time, have found in the Word a wellspring of truth and life.

Language and cultural barriers likewise can hinder engagement with Scripture, as translations may sometimes struggle to convey nuances or contextual meanings. Seek out multiple versions and commentaries and engage with teachers versed in original languages and historical contexts to understand God's Word better. The text of the Bible remains static; one's life circumstances do not. Therefore, one may confront the issue of drawing sustenance from Scripture in all seasons of life. It behooves believers to approach the Word with the conviction that it speaks as much to seasons of joy as to those of sorrow, to times of certainty as to those of searching.

Discouragement, too, can emerge when transformation seems to tarry despite diligent study. It is vital to recognize that the Word is like a seed sown in soil; the growth it beckons often occurs beneath the surface before it emerges for all to see.

Individuals may stumble in the endeavor to memorize Scripture, finding retention challenging. Yet, the consistent effort of hiding God's Word in one's heart is a worthy pursuit, nurturing an inner storehouse of wisdom ready for the Spirit's recall at necessary moments.

Specific passages in Scripture may elicit discomfort as they confront or confound conventional wisdom or personal convictions. When facing such texts, hold fast to a posture of humility, seeking to understand rather than to dismiss, and remain open to the transformation that often follows challenge.

For those grappling with guilt or unworthiness when approaching sacred text, it is crucial to recall that Scripture is a refuge for sinners, not a reward for saints. In its pages, one is meant to find grace, not grounds for self-condemnation.

Occasionally, believers can succumb to the temptation of reading Scripture superficially while treating devotion as a mere task to check off a daily list. Combat this by engaging with the Word as a dialogue with God, inviting His presence to permeate the reading and to speak through the sacred letters.

Lastly, Scripture may sometimes seem silent in the face of pressing questions or earnest prayers for guidance. In such seasons, persist in reading and reflection, trusting that in God's perfect timing, clarity shall come, and the silent Word shall resound with the answers sought.

Indeed, the challenges in connecting deeply with Scripture are manifold, yet with steadfast resolve, patient endurance, and the guiding light of the Holy Spirit, believers shall find in the Holy Bible an anchor amidst the storm, a compass in the wilderness, and a wellspring of living water in the arid landscapes of life.

Chapter 4:
Grace and Transformation

In the wake of understanding that grace truly is God's unmerited favor, and having anchored ourselves in the Word as our spiritual compass, we now turn to the transformative power of that grace in our lives. It's the kind of profound metamorphosis that can't be mistaken for mere self-improvement or willpower; it's a deep-rooted change that courses through our very being.

As grace empowers holiness within us, sanctification becomes the beautiful, ongoing journey we commit to, not as a burdensome task but as a joy-filled response to the love poured out upon us. And as we navigate this earthly life, the Word stands as an invaluable tool, helping us to meditate on the divine truths that shape our every action and thought. It equips us to be reflections of God's love, to live out our days with a purpose that far transcends our mere existence. In this dance of divinity, grace choreographs the steps of transformation, inviting us to participate fully in the divine plan that's both liberating and life-giving.

Grace Empowers Holiness

In the continuing journey of understanding grace and its vital role in our transformation, we realize that grace isn't just about forgiveness but empowerment. The grace of God isn't a passive gift; rather, it animates and invigorates our pursuit of holiness. When grace touches our hearts, it also reshapes our desires, aligning them more closely with God's heart.

Through this sanctifying grace, we're not merely avoiding wrongdoing but actively being drawn into the light of Christlikeness. In these moments, as grace fuels our discernment and strengthens our will, we truly begin to live lives set apart that willingly and joyously thrive under God's loving dominion. Holiness isn't a lofty ideal out of reach; it's the natural fruit borne when we allow grace to be the soil where our spirits grow.

The Process of Sanctification: In our journey through the ennobling vistas of grace and the foundational role of the Word in our lives, we understand that sanctification is the exquisite work of God in which we become active in our spiritual formation. Yet, to grasp how this transformative process occurs, we must first recognize that sanctification is not merely a moment in time but a lifelong pursuit.

Sanctification occurs through the continuous operation of divine grace in us. It is akin to the steady, patient erosion of old landscapes and the rising of new terrains within the human soul. It's about becoming more like Christ, enabling our behavior to align with God's will through the guidance of the Holy Spirit and a committed engagement with Scripture.

Spiritual disciplines play a vital role in the process of sanctification. These include prayer, fasting, worship, and the reading and meditation upon Scripture. As one engages in these practices, the heart is softened, the mind is renewed, and the individual's actions begin to reflect the righteousness of Christ.

Sanctification isn't passive; it necessitates human effort. While it's by grace that we are saved and by grace that we are sanctified, our response to this grace is critical. We must decide to pursue holiness, to yield to God's shaping hands, and to cooperate with the transformative work only He can accomplish in us.

Let's also clarify what sanctification is not—it's not a path to perfection in a fallen world. We won't achieve a state of sinlessness in this lifetime, for our mortal nature still binds us. However, sanctification involves ongoing repentance and an earnest striving against sin. This, in itself, is an act of God's grace at work within us.

Community is also essential in this process. By walking alongside others who share our pursuit of holiness, we find support, encouragement, and accountability. The church isn't simply a gathering of individuals but a collective force in sanctification, urging one another towards love and good deeds.

Fruitfulness is an outcome of sanctification. As we grow in grace, the fruits of the Spirit should become increasingly evident in our lives. Love, joy, peace, patience, kindness, goodness, faithfulness, gentleness, and self-control are markers of a life submitting to God's sanctifying work.

Trials and suffering, too, serve a role in our sanctification. They are, although perplexing at times, tools in the hands of an almighty God to mold and perfect our faith, producing perseverance. God uses these experiences in His sovereignty to refine us, strip away what is unclean, and draw us closer to Him.

Sanctification also involves a proper understanding of our identity in Christ. As we immerse ourselves in the truth of the Word, we see ourselves as God sees us: redeemed, called, and set apart. This understanding fuels our desire to live a life worthy of the calling we have received.

An increasing sensitivity to sin also marks the process of sanctification. As the light of Christ shines more brightly in us, areas of darkness are exposed—not to shame us, but to heal us. It is the kindness of the Lord that leads us to repentance, not a fear of condemnation.

Within sanctification lies the call to mission. As we are conformed to the image of Christ, his love compels us to reach out to others, to serve, and to share the good news of the grace by which we all may be saved. Sanctification is as much about being sent as it is about being set apart.

Worship is integral to sanctification. In prayer, we fix our eyes on Jesus, the author and perfecter of our faith, and as we gaze upon His glory, we are transformed. In the moments of heartfelt adoration, the Spirit works within us to change us from one degree of glory to another.

To those who might grow weary in their pursuit of sanctification, be heartened by the assurance that God works in you to will and to act to fulfill His good purpose. He who began a good work in you will continue until the day of Christ Jesus.

In conclusion, sanctification is a marvelous blend of divine initiative and human response. It requires our earnest effort and yet rests upon His empowering grace. It is a journey marked by the Word, walked in community, tested by trials, and celebrated in worship.

The grandeur of sanctification is that it prepares us for eternity. While we may see a dim reflection in a mirror now, the day is coming when we shall see face to face. Until that day, let us press on to take hold of that for which Christ Jesus took hold of us, embracing sanctification as the necessary travail and the glorious privilege of the Christian life.

Living a Holy Life through Grace In the preceding pages, we've traversed through the beauty and necessity of grace, allowing it to permeate the very essence of our belief system. Embarking from there, it becomes essential to unpack the practicality of grace as it pertains to the pursuit of holiness in one's life—a process not merely dependent on human effort but significantly enabled by divine grace.

Scripture heralds a call to holiness, for it is written, "Be holy because I am holy." This command appears as a daunting summit to scale, especially when met with the frailty of our nature. Yet, holiness is not a mark of spiritual elitism, nor a trophy of righteousness earned by toil. It is instead a state we're beckoned into, upheld by the tender graces of a loving God. For it's by grace we're saved, and by grace, we are transformed.

Understanding the framework laid by grace starts with recognizing its role as a catalyst for inner change. Many believers' strains under the weight of self-imposed expectations, trying to win God's favor. This is a fundamental misunderstanding, as grace comes precisely because we cannot make ourselves acceptable in God's eyes. Grace invites us into a transformative relationship, reassuring us that we don't have to earn what has been freely given.

Grace ushers us into the divine presence, where we find mercy and help in our quest for holiness. It's like sunlight to a plant—necessary for growth and impossible to generate on our own. In grace, we're not left to navigate the waters of morality by our compass; we are given the Holy Spirit, who leads and strengthens us in pursuing purity.

As we immerse ourselves in the Word of God, we don't merely ingest static text but interact with the living voice of the Holy One. The Word, which became flesh and dwelt among us, continues working within us. Through scripture, we learn not just about God but from God, exposing our hearts to the transforming influence of His Spirit.

The concept of sanctification introduces us to a lifelong journey. It is both instantaneous in our justification and progressive in our walk with Christ. The grace that pardons our sin at salvation is the same grace that empowers us to overcome sin each day after. It reveals that our sanctification is not labor finished in a day but achieved in the steady progression of a life surrendered.

Often, we might find ourselves discouraged by our faltering steps, but grace speaks louder than failure. It reaches down to lift us from despair, setting our feet upon the rock. In these moments, it's crucial to remember that grace never condones sin; instead, it equips us to defeat it. It reminds us that our worth is not in our perfection but Christ's atonement.

A question then may arise: how does one live with such grace? It begins with humble recognition—a transparent admission of our inherent weakness. For when we are weak, we're made strong through His grace. We call upon the Lord in our deficiencies and find His power perfected in our imperfections. It's a daily relinquishing of self, opening the heart to divine guidance.

The church, throughout generations, has witnessed the fruits of grace in the lives of those pursuing holiness. Such saints didn't boast of their righteousness but echoed the dependency on grace that fueled their virtues. Their stories linger not as unreachable lore but as encouragement that grace is efficacious in the mundane and meaningful.

Prayers, therefore, become a vital communication, not of wishing, but of receiving. We approach the throne of grace, bringing our need for holiness before God, confident that we'll receive mercy and find grace to help us exactly when needed. Engaging in prayer, Scripture reading, and communion helps maintain our connection to the power source of our holiness—God Himself.

A life of holiness is also marked by its fruits—expressions of love, joy, peace, patience, kindness, goodness, faithfulness, gentleness, and self-control. These are not virtues to be mustered by sheer will but ones that flow naturally out of a life aligned by grace. They are evidence of the Spirit at work, shaping our desires and deeds to reflect the holiness of our Creator.

Grace also equips us to confront sin unequivocally. While grace covers all transgressions, it also gives us the resolve and resources to resist temptation and live rightly. Therein lies a delicate balance: acknowledging grace's forgiveness yet striving to sin no more. Through grace, we receive the discernment and fortitude to turn away from sin and toward godliness.

Walking in obedience becomes a joy, not a chore when we comprehend that grace is our starting line and the track we run on. It frees us from legalism and empowers us to live according to God's ways because our desire to obey grows from gratitude rather than obligation—an overflow of the loving relationship established and maintained by grace.

In navigating life's labyrinth with its moral dualities and complexities, grace becomes our ethical compass. It provides clarity and encourages us not to conform to this world but to be transformed by renewing our minds. It shapes our moral imagination, enabling us to envision life through the lens of Christ's righteousness and inspiring us to emulate Him in action and thought.

Living a holy life, therefore, is not an abstruse concept reserved for the ascetic or the saintly—it's an accessible reality for every child of God, powered by the inexhaustible grace of our Lord. Then, with confidence, let us draw near to the throne of grace so that we may receive mercy and find grace to help in times of need and pursue holiness, not as a burdensome duty but as a divine gift and calling.

The Word as a Tool for Spiritual Growth

In the journey toward spiritual maturity, the Word is not simply a body of knowledge but a dynamic instrument of change. As believers yearn for deeper communion with the Divine, scripture sustains that profound hunger—a hunger that can't be sated by earthly means. Within its living pages, the Bible reveals itself to be more than a sacred text; it is an active participant in the believer's transformation.

Engaging in the spiritual discipline of meditating on scripture cultivates an inner garden from which fruits of righteousness may sprout. Applying what one learns from these divine revelations to everyday life ensures that behavior aligns with belief, resulting in a faith that isn't static but one that breathes, evolves, and thrives amid life's manifold trials. Thus, God's Word becomes both the map and the compass for the soul's pilgrimage, guiding and nurturing believers as they walk the path of grace toward ever-increasing glory.

Meditating on Scripture

The tapestry of our spiritual lives is often woven in the quiet corners where the heart and Scripture meet. Meditating on Scripture, a pivotal tool for spiritual growth involves rumination on the divine truths encapsulated in the Bible. Unlike the oft-perceived notions of meditation that dwell on emptying the mind, Christian meditation is about filling the mind with the Word of God, allowing His Spirit to inform and transform our innermost beings.

Indeed, the biblical injunction to meditate on Scripture Day and night, as noted in Joshua 1:8, is not a suggestion but a command. It speaks to the vitality of this practice in everyday living. Meditating on the Word is both a discipline and a delight, a place where discipline yields to devotion until His words resonate in us, through us, and from us.

Meditation begins with selecting a portion of Scripture. One might choose a verse or a passage that speaks to their current circumstances or calls out to their Spirit for deeper understanding. Approach the text with reverence, understanding this is not merely a book but the very breath of God rendered in language we can comprehend.

Reading the Scripture gently and repeatedly opens the door to more profound insight. As the words are softly spoken or silently pondered, they marinate in the heart. This slow procession of words across the chasms of our souls allows the Holy Spirit to highlight truths, draw out wisdom, and awaken understanding.

Reflection then ensues, not a passive action but an active engagement with the text. To reflect upon a passage invites questions, considers its implications, and draws connections to one's life. Mediation matures in this active reflection, taking root in our conscience and flourishing in our daily decisions.

One mustn't rush through this spiritual exercise. The goal is not to tick off a checklist or to conquer chapters. Meditation is savoring, not skimming; it's about depth, not necessarily breadth. As you dwell in God's presence with an open Bible, time becomes secondary to the timeless truths unfolding before you.

As the psalmist delightfully declares in Psalm 1, one who meditates on God's law is like a tree planted by streams of water, yielding fruit in season. Think of your soul as that tree and the Scripture as the nourishing waters. With each meditation session, roots grow deeper, faith strengthens, and fruits of the Spirit become abundant in one's character.

If barriers arise, such as distraction or dryness, view them not as defeat but as opportunities to depend more fully upon God's grace. Ask for the Spirit's guidance and restoration of focus. Remember, even saints of old encountered distractions in their pursuit of divine intimacy. It's the continual return to the Word that triumphs over wandering thoughts.

Visualize the words of Scripture and let them form images and scenarios in your mind's eye. Imagine the biblical scenes, empathize with the characters, and insert yourself into the narrative. This exercise makes the text relive in your heart and helps apply its truths to your current context.

Allow meditation to segue into prayer. Respond to God's Word with your words, whether it be a prayer of thanks, a request for wisdom, or a plea for strength. Scripture fuels our conversation with God; through it, we can ascertain His will and seek alignment with His purposes.

Indeed, meditating on Scripture is not an isolated event but is connected intrinsically to living out the Word. As one meditates, the truths gleaned should imbue one's actions, decisions, and interactions with others. Thus, the divine becomes not just a portion of life but permeates the entirety of our living.

Regular mediation fortifies one's spiritual armor. Ephesians 6 reminds us that the Word is our sword of the Spirit, ready to defend against deception, temptation, and despondence. Hence, anchoring ourselves in the living Word through meditation prepares us for daily spiritual battles.

Meditation on Scripture is also an act of worship, acknowledging that God's Word is worthy of our full attention and reflective thought. It's a posture of humility, recognizing the need for divine wisdom that surpasses our understanding and transforms our will to align with His.

Let us, therefore, embrace the sacred rhythm of meditating on God's Word. In the silent chambers of a meditative heart, His voice, gentle and steadfast, shapes the melodies of our lives. May our meditation be sweet and our delight in His Word be evident in every facet of our journey.

In conclusion, meditating on Scripture is not a mere accessory to the Christian faith but a vital organ pulsating at its center. It captivates our minds, enriches our hearts, and sets our spirits in tune with the very heart of God. May we be diligent in this practice and reap the fruits of a life deeply rooted in the eternal truths of Scripture.

Apply God's Word to Everyday Life

As we delve into the application of God's Word in daily life's bustle, we must recognize that Scripture is not a mere collection of abstract theories or distant tales. Instead, it serves as a mirror and map—reflecting who we are and guiding us to who we are called to be. With each step we take, and our decisions, the spiritual wisdom distilled in the Bible proves relevant and essential.

In the workplace, the principles of Scripture guide us toward integrity and diligence. The Proverbs laud the merits of hard work and warn against the pitfalls of shortcuts and deception. To apply this, one might choose to complete tasks with excellence, regardless of who's supervising, or to speak truthfully in meetings, even when embellishing could be tempting.

In our homes, the command to love our neighbors as ourselves starts with those closest to us. It can be as simple and challenging as practicing patience with our children, extending forgiveness to a spouse, or providing care for an aging parent. These acts of service reflect the love detailed in 1 Corinthians 13—a love that is patient and kind and keeps no record of wrongs.

Financial decisions also provide an opportunity to apply biblical wisdom. God's Word speaks volumes about the use of money, directing us not towards hoarding but generosity, not to greed but contentment. For instance, one might set up a regular plan for giving to those in need or to their local church, recognizing that God gives all we possess and is to be used for His glory.

The call to bear one another's burdens becomes a daily practice in personal relationships. This might look like being there for a friend during tough times, offering a listening ear or a shoulder to lean on, thus living out Jesus's compassionate love.

Scripture guides us to seek peace and reconciliation rather than vengeance or grudge-holding when confronted with conflict. This could mean initiating a difficult conversation to mend a strained relationship, drawing on the wisdom of Matthew 18, which outlines steps for resolving disputes among believers.

Even in our leisure, the Word provides perspective. It teaches us to enjoy the gifts God has given us but to do so in a manner that honors Him. We learn balance, avoiding the twin pitfalls of asceticism on the one hand and hedonism on the other. Whether it's rest, recreation, or creative pursuits, our faith can align with and inspire our activities.

Navigating the societal challenges of our day, the Scripture acts as a beacon of truth and justice. It propels us to engage with issues of injustice and poverty, not as distant spectators but as active participants in God's redemptive work. Thus, aligning with prophets like Micah, we strive to act justly, love mercy, and walk humbly with God.

The Word also informs our personal growth and discipline. The epistles offer encouragement and instruction for those seeking to cultivate self-control or break free from harmful habits. Intentionally pursuing such virtues is a sprawling journey of becoming Christ-like in our thoughts and actions.

In moments of anxiety or despair, Scripture does not leave us comfortless. The Psalms provide a blueprint for pouring our sorrows to God while reminding us of His faithful presence. In this way, we are encouraged to bring our whole selves to God—joy, pain, hope, and fear.

At times of celebration and joy, the Word encourages us to remember the source of all blessings. By fostering a heart of gratitude and praise, we echo David's psalms and mirror the attitude of thankfulness portrayed throughout Scripture, thereby keeping our hearts attuned to God's grace.

As life presents big and small decisions, the Spirit of wisdom that permeates the Word can guide our choices. From daily routines to life-altering changes, we encounter the chance to live out principles taught by Jesus in the Sermon on the Mount—seeking first the kingdom of God in all things.

Communal life is enriched when we view our interactions through the lens of Scripture. In church, social gatherings, or volunteer activities, we aim to demonstrate the unity and love among believers that Jesus prayed for in John 17. Our shared commitment to Christ becomes the cornerstone of a meaningful community.

Finally, when we face the inevitable losses and griefs of this life, the comfort we receive from God through His Word is not meant to be hoarded. 2 Corinthians 1 reminds us that we are comforted so that we may comfort others. Thus, the application of Scripture comes full circle, extending the compassion and comfort we have received.

Adorned with the wisdom of the ages contained within the sacred text, we are beckoned to live lives that are not merely our own but reflections of the One we serve. Through each interaction, choice, and moment of reflection, we inhale the breath of Scripture and exhale the life of faith—making the presence of Christ known in our world. In this way, God's Word becomes not just a light unto our path but also a light through us to the paths of others.

Chapter 5:
Grace and Relationships

Having traversed the transformative power of grace and its ability to sanctify our beings, we now turn our attention to the profound impact this grace has within the sphere of our interpersonal relationships. When grace permeates our interactions, it fosters an atmosphere where forgiveness is not only possible but becomes a natural spill-over of the mercy we ourselves have received.

It is through this divine framework that rifts are healed, and understanding is deepened. The Scriptures are not silent on these matters; they serve as a guiding light, highlighting how we are to conduct ourselves in love, mirroring the sacrificial love of Christ. In this chapter, we delve into the intertwining of grace with relationships, considering God's Word as our steadfast counsel in nurturing healthy, grace-filled connections with others, reflecting the harmony and unity intended by our Creator.

Grace-Fueled Forgiveness

As an act of gratefulness, forgiveness is a powerful expression of grace mixed within the complex structure that makes up our relationships and lives. It is a concept that matters much for people who have taken on the power of redemption because it's no longer simply an option but something personal reinforced by God's love.

In this process, we are also compelled to overcome our earthly inclinations to hold onto grudges and instead provide empathy and forgiveness to those who have wronged us, just as we say in the LORD's Prayer. This is a profound demonstration of goodwill and has the power to transform deep reservoirs of animosity into healing, restoration, and reconciliation. Astonishingly, God's mercy releases us from the chains of our past transgressions and unites us with a harmonious future full of harmony and reconciliation.

Forgiving Others as We Are Forgiven

Forgiveness is the scaffold upon which our understanding of grace is built. It is the act that emulates God's boundless mercy toward us and reflects it in the mirror of our human interactions. In the tapestry of Christian life, threads of forgiveness intertwine with those of love, creating a pattern that reveals the divine image in each of us. The instruction is explicit, as we daily aver in the Lord's Prayer: 'Forgive us our debts, as we also have forgiven our debtors.'

To forgive others as we are forgiven is no facile task; it is a divine command that challenges the depths of our souls. It is an aspiration that can only be fulfilled through the empowering work of God's Spirit within us. Our prime example is Christ, who, while nailed unjustly to the cross, found the voice to petition: 'Father, forgive them, for they do not know what they are doing.' Such an utterance seems beyond human capacity, yet it is the standard set before us.

Forgiveness is not a mere dismissal of wrongdoing or ignoring the hurt caused. It is a deliberate choice to release the other from the debt they owe us as a result of their actions. It does not permit continued wrongs nor deny the need for justice or repentance. On the contrary, it seeks the reconciliation and redemption that can only arise from a heart aligned with God's heart.

When we harbor unforgiveness, it is as if we chain ourselves to the very thing God has freed us from. Resentment becomes a malignancy in our spirit, hindering our prayers, clouding our vision, and preventing the entire flow of grace. It's an unnecessary burden that we're called to lay down at the foot of Christ's cross, where the greatest act of forgiveness was bestowed upon humanity.

Forgiving others is not a solitary event but a lifelong journey. It often demands our humility and requires us to relinquish our pride. This path may be painful to tread, as it invites us to remember our brokenness and our profound need for God's merciful grace. Thus, forgiving others reminds us of the outstanding debt dismissed for our trespasses.

Frequently, the act of forgiveness requires us to have a strength we did not know we possessed, which comes from the empowering of the Holy Spirit. It is an act of warfare against the powers of darkness that seek to keep us in bondage to bitterness and strife. There is a triumph in the release of forgiveness, a victory that mirrors the resurrection power of Christ, breaking the chains of sin and death.

Understanding forgiveness necessitates a grasp of God's nature. God is just, and sin cannot be overlooked or considered trivial. It required a substantial sacrifice, the gift of His Son, to bridge the chasm sin had wrought between God and humanity. Likewise, when we forgive others, we recognize the gravity of the offense yet choose to cover it with love, reflecting the very essence of God's character.

Forgiveness also protects the unity of the Body of Christ. The Word affirms that a house divided against itself cannot stand. In light of this, forgiveness becomes a personal act and a communal imperative. The oil soothes friction and maintains the integrity of relationships within the community of believers. For where there is forgiveness, there is harmony that allows the Spirit of God to move freely.

There is wisdom in understanding that forgiveness does not equate to putting oneself back in harm's way. It does not demand we re-enter a situation or relationship where ongoing injury is inevitable. Instead, it may necessitate healthy boundaries even as the heart releases unforgiveness. Discernment is key in navigating the landscapes of forgiveness, knowing when reconciliation is possible and when it is not.

Forgiving others as we are forgiven becomes an expression of trust in God. It acknowledges God's sovereignty in justice and leaves the ultimate righting of wrongs in His capable hands. We forgive, not because we deny the wrongness of the action against us, but because we hold to a God more significant than any wound inflicted upon us.

Nonetheless, forgiveness is not merely a personal or individual practice; it bears witness to the grace we have received. In forgiving others, we become ambassadors of reconciliation, testifying to the world of the hope that lies within us. Our act of forgiveness speaks volumes, revealing the Gospel's transformative power.

In practical terms, the journey of forgiveness often starts with a decision, not a feeling. It is a choice to speak blessings over those who curse us and to pray for those who mistreat us. It is a daily discipline that aligns our hearts with God's, gradually transforming bitterness into compassion and anger into peace. It is, at times, a process that does not align with our instincts, and yet, it is a process that leads us to spiritual freedom.

Ultimately, in our endeavor to forgive others as we are forgiven, we encounter the vastness of God's grace. We behold the beauty of the Gospel in a new light, appreciating the depths of love displayed at Calvary. As we extend grace to others, we also experience it anew, realizing that in God's economy, forgiveness is a gift to the recipient and the giver.

In the quiet moments of surrender, when our hearts yield to God's prompting to forgive, we experience Christ's profound peace. Letting go of the right to hold onto grudges, we embrace the freedom purchased through Christ's sacrifice. It is here, in these acts of mercy, that our souls discover the path to true healing and wholeness.

In the fabric of Christian living, the thread of forgiveness may be difficult to weave, yet it is indispensable to the strength and beauty of the finished work. We forgive because we are profoundly aware of our own need for grace. And in this sacred duty, we honor the Lord who forgave us and called us to live in the freedom of His grace, reflecting His love to a world in desperate need of both.

Healing Broken Relationships Through the lenses of grace and the wisdom of the Scriptures, we find ample direction for mending the fractures within our interpersonal connections. Healing comes not solely from our efforts but relies on the divine interventions of grace and the discerning guidance of God's Word. Relationships weathered by discord, miscommunication, or harm need a balm that can only come from acknowledging brokenness and a deep yearning for reconciliation.

The endeavor to repair a broken relationship must often begin with forgiveness. This cardinal virtue, depicted thoroughly in the Scriptures, forms the bedrock upon which fractured connections can find renewal. To forgive as our Lord has forgiven us is a divine command that necessitates humility and abundant grace. It can be an arduous journey that commences within the human heart, calling it out of the darkness of anger and resentment and into the light of love and understanding.

The pursuit of honest, clear communication is equally crucial in the healing process. Word compels us to speak the truth in love, to convey our feelings and grievances without coating them in bitterness or malice. As we navigate the treacherous waters of reconciliation, let us shun fraught silence and instead seek to express our hearts with transparency, inviting God's wisdom to lead our words and our listening.

Patience is integral to healing broken relationships. Appropriating grace in our interactions means allowing time for wounds to heal and rebuilding trust. Healing cannot be rushed; like the dawn breaking gently over the horizon, it arrives in its time. We must bear with one another and forbear, understanding that restoration is often a gradual process, respecting the pace at which others mend.

As we seek restoration, humility must undergird our every action. Recognizing our failings, seeking forgiveness, and being willing to change are all critical aspects of mending what has frayed. An honest self-assessment, acknowledging our role in the discord, is often the first step toward genuine change.

Accountability, a principle strongly upheld by the Word, plays a vital role. By holding ourselves and others responsible for our actions and their consequences, we stand against the recurrence of harmful patterns. Accountability is not an avenue for finger-pointing but a pathway to ensure mutual respect and honor moving forward.

Seeking wisdom through prayer is an indispensable part of healing. The Scriptures assure us that when we lack wisdom, we can ask of God, who gives generously without finding fault. In our struggle to mend broken ties, we must turn to prayer, soliciting Heaven's aid for insight and strength.

We must also remember to extend grace to ourselves and those we seek to reconcile with. Just as Christ has graciously received us, so must we receive each other, laying down our rights and pride to lift the banner of peace.

Confronting the issues that led to disunity is inevitable. The Word instructs us that wisdom is to recognize a matter in its true nature. As we confront, let it be with a spirit of gentleness and a firm resolve to seek solutions, not merely to unearth past grievances. It becomes an opportunity to address the root causes and to heal profound and unattended hurts.

Throughout this journey, community plays a key role. The church body, a haven of shared belief and commitment, provides support, counsel, and prayer. Surrounding ourselves with fellow believers who share our values and faith in Christ's redemptive power can strengthen us in our quest for reconciliation.

It is salient to pursue wisdom and discernment anew each day. The Scriptures serve as a mirror reflecting the areas in our relationships that require work and as a light guiding our steps toward healing. Like any rigorous journey, the path toward repaired relationships is dotted with moments of clarity, hardship, and immense hope.

When relationships find healing, it testifies to the transformative power of grace at work in our lives. It becomes a chance to demonstrate the radical love that Christ has shown us, a love not conditioned on perfection but on sincere endeavor and grace-filled interaction. These restored relationships then stand as evidence, not of our goodness, but of God's abiding presence in our lives.

In conclusion, let us not shy away from the complex tapestry of human relationships, for even in their brokenness, they hold the possibility of revealing the depths of God's grace. Through forgiveness, communication, patience, humility, accountability, prayer, and community, our relationships can be woven anew with the threads of divine love. And as we faithfully adhere to the precepts found in the Word, we shall discover the strength and wisdom needed for restoration.

May anyone embarking on the quest of healing broken relationships be undergirded by God's boundless grace and guided by the eternal truth of His Word. The journey may be arduous, but the destination—reconciliation and peace—resounds with the harmony of Heaven itself. To those walking this path: may you find solace in the knowledge that your efforts are seen, your tears known, and your desire for unity deeply echoes the heart of the Father.

The Word's Guidance in Our Interactions

As we have explored the depths of grace and how it compels us to extend forgiveness, we now turn to the manner in which the Word enlightens the pathways of our personal interactions. Scripture is not merely a collection of ancient texts; rather, it's a living conduit through which God's voice shapes our relationships.

It's in the everyday encounters, those moments steeped in the mundane and the monumental, that we find the Word's guidance crucial. Biblical principles become the plumb line for conduct, calling us to love selflessly, communicate truthfully, and serve humbly. By imitating Christ's relational model, we forge connections that not only endure but also become testaments of divine love and the transformative power of grace in our lives.

Biblical Principles for Healthy Relationships

In the journey through this treatise, we've discerned how grace and the Word undergird every facet of our lives. As we turn to the context of relationships, we must knit these principles closely with our interactions. In the Bible, we observe that relationships are not merely addenda to our faith walk—they are their very essence. Where grace meets our relational sphere, it demands that we extend the same tolerance and kindness lavished upon us.

The foremost principle threading through Scripture's narrative on relationships is love, as seen in 1 Corinthians 13:1-13. Not the temporary, emotion-driven love of secular tunes but the agape love—a selfless, sacrificial love that seeks the highest good of the other, irrespective of merit. This love doesn't germinate from our impoverished reservoirs; it overflows from the abundance we have received through Christ. Even if a conflict exists, it should not be your fault, or you should not be the reason it lingers because the Bible also says, "If it is possible, as far as it depends on you, live at peace with everyone" (Romans 12:18).

As we contemplate love, we can't overlook the golden rule of conduct, which says: "Do to others as you would have them do to you" (Luke 6:31). This timeless precept encapsulates the ethics of Christ's kingdom, beckoning us to look beyond our desires and consider the well-being of our neighbor. It echoes the sage wisdom that love is not merely a sentiment but an action—a series of choices made in the best interest of another.

Another bedrock principle found within the sacred pages is forgiveness. A life touched by grace cannot clutch grudges. We all stumble, and offenses are inevitable in the labyrinth of human relations. Yet, it is through forgiveness that relationships are mended and restored. In forgiving, we untether ourselves from the anchorage of past wrongs and set sail toward reconciliation—mirroring the divine forgiveness bestowed upon us.

Transparency is likewise essential in nurturing healthy relationships. Authenticity breeds trust, and trust is the cornerstone of any thriving relationship. The biblical call for truth-telling and honest living is not merely prophylactic against deception; it is a clarion call for integrity—an invitation to live so that our words and actions align under the scrutiny of God's light.

Boundaries, too, are significant. Discernment, which flows from immersion in the Word, protects us from relationships that can lead us astray. Just as Nehemiah rebuilt the walls of Jerusalem for its protection, so must we build healthy boundaries to foster and safeguard our personal and communal well-being.

Humility holds sway in how we relate to one another. Changing the dichotomy from dominance to service, just as Christ "did not come to be served, but to serve" (Mark 10:45), we must adopt a posture of humility in our associations. This includes the readiness to admit wrongdoing, the grace to place others above oneself, and the tranquility to be serene in the face of misunderstanding or contempt.

We are urged to bear each other's burdens, aligning with Paul's exhortation that such acts fulfill the law of Christ (Galatians 6:2). The practice of compassion positions us into the reality of others, allowing us to become vessels through which God's comfort and solace are channeled. It involves an active participation in the sorrows and joys of those around us, binding us together in an unspoken fellowship of the Spirit.

Encouragement is another filament that strengthens the fabric of healthy relationships. In a world of disparagement and despair, words of encouragement act as beacons of hope. Scripture calls us to edify one another, be mindful that the power of life and death is in the tongue, and use our words to uplift rather than tear down.

In a tapestry of diverse gifts and callings, unity is not found in uniformity but in harmonious diversity. The early church, as described in the Acts of the Apostles, reveals how unity flourished amid diversity through the shared commitment to a common cause. Relationships flourish when each person's uniqueness is acknowledged and celebrated, contributing to the intricate mosaic of God's family.

The practice of patience is another virtue indispensable for harmonious relationships. Rather than insisting on immediate fulfillment or understanding, patience allows for growth and change—

the same long-suffering patience God exhibits toward us in our waywardness and stumbling.

Lastly, it behooves us to nurture the soil of our relationships with the living waters of prayer. The humble act of interceding for one another binds us in ways that transcend human understanding, reinforcing the spiritual ligaments that unite the Body of Christ.

In conclusion, healthy relationships are not lucky—they are cultivated through the deliberate application of biblical precepts in our daily lives. Let us endeavor to weave these principles together, creating a tapestry that honors the One who calls us into loving fellowship with Himself and one another.

What remains now is to live out these scriptural tenets, applying them with grace-filled hearts. May we be conscious of the divine image within each individual, fostering respect and dignity in our interactions. And when we fall short, as we undoubtedly will, let us hasten to the wellspring of grace, where our relationships can be cleansed, healed, and made whole again.

Through these principles, our relationships will not only survive the tumults of life but will thrive, exhibiting to the world the beauty and wisdom of a life centered on the precepts of Scripture. Let us hold fast to the Word, which guides us, and the grace, which sustains us, as we build and maintain relationships that reflect the heart of our Creator.

Love One Another as Christ Loved Us

To love as Christ loved is a high, holy calling that pierces the very essence of our being and transforms our interactions into manifestations of divine grace. Upon this cornerstone of Christian practice, we build relationships that reflect the splendor of our Savior's selfless affection.

What does it mean to love as He loved us? Christ's love was sacrificial, unselfish, and proactive. He sought out those in need, healed the hurting and offered hope to the hopeless. His entire being was directed towards the welfare of others, setting a transcendent example for us to emulate.

Such love cannot be conjured up by mere human effort; it must flow from a heart that God's unconditional love has changed. When we grasp the depth of Jesus' sacrifice for us and understand that He died not because we deserved it but precisely because we did not, this humbling revelation begins to reshape our hearts. It urges us to extend the same unmerited love to those around us.

As we wade deeper into the waters of Christ's love, we must confront our natural tendencies toward selfishness and pride. These are the scourges that mar our ability to love as He loved. They make us hoard, not offer; they make us judge, not embrace; they make us build walls, not bridges.

Yet, we aren't left to fight these battles alone. The Scripture is both our guide and strength in this pursuit. Through the Word, we can understand love's proper form. 1 Corinthians 13 paints love not as a fleeting feeling but as a set of actions and decisions—patience, kindness, protection, trust, hope, and perseverance.

In the practical outworking of our faith, this means prioritizing others' needs, forgiving without limit, and seeking reconciliation. It calls for a shift from a me-centered life to an other-centered life, a life generously poured out for the benefit of others.

The principle of loving one another also fundamentally shifts the dynamics of our relationships. Within the family, it creates a nurturing environment where each member feels valued and cherished. Among friends, it fosters deep trust and genuine connection. Even towards our enemies, this principle challenges us to act in love, blessing those who curse us and praying for those who mistreat us.

But such radical love is not merely about grand gestures but daily choices. It's about listening attentively, speaking words of encouragement, and offering our time, resources, and companionship without seeking something in return.

This love is also a healing balm. It's an agent of restoration that can repair the breaches caused by misunderstandings, disagreements, and deep hurts. By loving as Christ did, we become conduits of His grace, offering others a chance to experience forgiveness, healing, and renewal.

Christ's love should also be mirrored in the way we handle conflict. It's about seeking peace, not being correct, about harmony, not victory. Such love encourages dialogue and understanding and is rooted in the desire for unity and fellowship.

The love of Christ knows no barriers of race, social status, or personal background. It is a love that embraces diversity and seeks to break down the dividing walls of hostility that too often separate us. In this love, there is neither Jew nor Greek, enslaved person nor free, but all are one in Christ Jesus.

For those called to leadership within the body of Christ, this mandate of love is especially pertinent. Leaders must not only teach and defend the faith but do so in a manner consistent with Christ's sacrificial love. It's about shepherding with gentleness, leading by example, and nurturing the flock with tender care.

Amidst the everyday bustle, losing sight of this divine call to love can be easy. Life's demands can make us insensitive to the needs around us. But remembering Jesus' command to love one another as

He has loved us brings us back to the heart of our Christian walk. This love is not optional; it's the essence of what it means to follow Christ.

To cultivate this Christlike love, prayer and reflection are indispensable. We must continually present our hearts before God, asking Him to fill us with His love, see others through His eyes, and give us the strength to extend grace even when it's hard.

Finally, let us be encouraged that while our efforts to love as Christ loved are imperfect, the divine love that works within us is not. It is His Spirit that empowers, His grace that motivates, and His love that ultimately heals and transforms. In Him, our tentative steps toward loving others are met with the abundant outpouring of His perfect love, which never fails.

Chapter 6:
Anchored in the Storm

In the midst of life's tempests, where waves thrash against the soul with unrelenting force, there exists a steadfast anchor that holds firm: the grace of God as revealed through His Word. Just as a ship caught in a gale finds refuge in the strength of its anchor, so we find our refuge in the promises scripted in the holy texts.

As we navigate the challenges life thrusts upon us, let us not be dismayed, for it isn't in the absence of adversity that our faith is proven, but in the throes of it. When we're beset by the winds of trials, it's the transformative grace that fortifies our spirits, allowing us to unearth strength where only weakness seemed to reside. Clinging to the Scriptures infuses our hearts with courage, as it is written, "The Lord is my strength and my shield." And in the sanctum of prayer, we find a solace that transcends human understanding, for it is there that we are in communion with the divine—an unequivocal source of comfort in our times of need.

Navigate Life's Challenges with Grace

Laden with the trials that buffet our lives like relentless waves, we might falter under the illusion that we're adrift alone. And yet, it's precisely within these tempests where grace emerges, not just as a lifeline but as the very winds that guide our sails towards tranquility.

Finding strength in our weaknesses becomes less a paradox and more a divine truth when we allow God's grace to seep into the fractures of our existence, mending and fortifying us from within. As Scripture affirms, it's not our might but God's power made perfect in our frailty that upholds us. To face our trials with faith, then, is like planting one's feet upon a rock amid the surging tides; by grace, we're anchored securely, weathering storms not just with endurance but with a poise that transcends mere survival, reaching into the realm of the serene and the sublime.

Finding Strength in Weakness

His strength is made perfect in our weakness (2 Corinthians 12:9). There speaks of the Apostle Paul, citing what Jesus said, "My grace is sufficient for you because My strength perfects itself in weakness." This is because God is perfect in all respects. He possesses the qualities within Himself to make up for whatever imperfections we may have had, even a ton of it.

In the contemplative journey through life's challenges, one often confronts a paradox that seems antithetical to human nature: that power surfaces most poignantly in moments of perceived frailty. How can we unearth a strength arguably more potent than the might of our fortune at its zenith in our weakest moments? This counterintuitive discovery is not merely a philosophical proposition but lies at the heart of grace as it intertwines with the Christian faith.

Strength in weakness is a recurring motif in the Scriptures, an intersecting point where divine grace collides with human inadequacy. It's within the depths of our insufficiency that grace performs its most profound work, redefining our limitations as the very platform for God's power. The Apostle Paul encapsulated this living contradiction when he relayed the words given to him, 'My grace is sufficient for you, for my power is made perfect in weakness.'

When we face insurmountable obstacles, emotions that overwhelm our equilibrium, and afflictions that threaten our peace, we are driven to the understanding that our capacities fall short. It's here, at this cliff edge of desperation, that grace extends itself. A lifeline not born of our crafting but one forged in the divine purpose that reorients our hearts towards reliance on power beyond our own.

Embracing our vulnerabilities does not necessitate resignation to defeat. Instead, it means actively accepting the reality of our human state while reaching out for the boundless grace that transcends it. This juxtaposition of acceptance and transcendence ushers us into a dance with humility, teaching us to let go of the ego and lay hold of something far more significant.

Weakness, too, refines our character. In the heat of difficulty, traits of patience, perseverance, and empathy are annealed within us, often unseen until the cooling waters of retrospection reveal the transformation. Within these formative years, grace kindles the beauty of Christ-like character fashioned in the furnace of our frailties.

Moreover, strength in weakness manifests as an instrument of testimony. Observers, seeing the extraordinary peace that dominates our demeanor amidst trials, can't help but recognize the source of our strength: grace itself. The narrative of our lives becomes a vibrant testament to the restorative power of grace working within us, a beacon to those sailing through their storms.

Grace also equips us to comfort others. Forged through our battles and branded by our experiences, we can stand alongside others in their struggles, offering a depth of understanding that only those who have tasted a similar bitterness yet found the sweetness of grace can offer.

We must also be rooted in the Word to find strength in weakness. In the pages of the Holy Scripture, we are reminded of the great cloud of witnesses who have walked before us, embodying this paradox. The

Scripture is laden with stories of the unlikely, the unqualified, and the underestimated, who accomplished the extraordinary when graced by God.

We are clinging to the Word in moments of weakness, which channels us the same assurances that fortified saints of old. As we meditate on the immovable truths of God, the whispers of our inadequacies are drowned out by the roaring reminder that we serve a God who relishes making the impossible possible.

Weakness also teaches us the rhythm of God's timing. In a world that idolizes instant solutions and immediate results, weakness slows us down, aligning our pace with the sometimes invisible, yet unstoppable, movement of God's workings in our lives.

Furthermore, we learn the art of surrender within the crucible of weakness. As we release our grip on control, it's grace that shapes our next steps, often into paths that we would not have chosen but that lead to vistas of growth and blessing unforeseen.

The strength that emerges from weakness is not a force that puffs up; it's a fortified gentleness, a powerful serenity. It's a portrayal not of a God who pulls us from our trials but of a God who enters into them with us, shouldering the burden and imbuing us with an inexplicable strength that carries us from moment to moment.

This strength, however, is not an end in itself. It is not my reliance on personal triumphs but on the improvement of the body of Christ. It serves to knit the believers together, each one's strength bolstering another's knees, each story of grace fortifying the faith of the fellowship.

As you navigate your seasons of weakness, know you are not called to shuffle through them unaided. You are invited to partake in a di ine exchange where your weakness is met with His strength, and your humility becomes the chalice into which grace is poured. In the quiet acknowledgment of our weakness, we can confidently say, as did Paul, 'When I am weak, then I am strong.'

Thus, finding strength in weakness is not just a vain hope but an assured promise. It is a paradoxical principle that lies at the beating heart of a life anchored in the Word and sponsored by grace—a spiritual axiom that, once apprehended, becomes profoundly liberating. In embracing our weakness, we do not capitulate to despair; instead, we lean into the everlasting arms of grace that upholds, sustains, and empowers us for the journey ahead.

Facing Trials with Faith

Faith is the rudder steering our ship amid life's storms, often invisibly beneath the surface. It's not about the absence of fear but the courage to move forward despite it. Trials are as old as humanity itself; they test the mettle of our souls and the depth of our belief. As we delve into understanding the profound relationship between faith and trials, it is crucial to acknowledge that faith is not merely a passive state but an active force within us, galvanizing our spirits in times of adversity.

Scripture accounts for individuals who faced staggering odds, like David before Goliath or Daniel in the lion's den. Their triumphs weren't born from their power but from an unwavering trust in the Almighty, which turns ordinary stones into mighty weapons and an imminent demise into a testimony of survival.

Amid our afflictions, wondering why a loving God would permit such hardships is tempting. Yet it's precisely through these trials that faith is refined and strengthened. Just as gold must endure the furnace to purge its impurities, so must our faith be tested to grow purer and more potent. This does not suggest that God takes pleasure in our suffering, but rather, He is committed to our ultimate good shaping us into the likeness of His Son.

Joseph's life is an embodiment of enduring trials with faith. Betrayal, false accusations, and imprisonment marked his path, but he remained steadfast. His unyielding faith became his triumph, placing him at Pharaoh's right hand, saving nations and restoring his family. Through his eyes, we learn that trials have the potential to guide us to our providential purpose if we remain anchored in faith.

Trials confront us with a choice: to retreat into the shadows of doubt or to take a stand on the bedrock of faith. Choosing faith means trusting God's character, unchanging nature, and promises. Consider the sparrow that does not sow or reap yet never goes unnoticed by our Heavenly Father. If His eye is on the sparrow, how much more is He attentive to those He calls His children?

Yet, we must be candid; faith does not grant us immunity from the sting of suffering. It does, however, arm us with a perspective that transcends our present pains. The Apostle Paul's thorn in the flesh is a testament to this. Each pleading for relief was met with a simple, profound promise: "My grace is sufficient for you, for my power is made perfect in weakness." Here is the paradox – God's strength is most potent within us in our most fragile moments.

How do we maintain our course in faith when the waves grow menacing? Firstly, we must be vigilant in prayer, for it is the lifeline that connects our frail hearts with divine power. To pray is not to recite empty words but to actively engage in a spiritual battle, using the weapon of our testimony, wielding the shield of faith, and securing victory in Christ's victory.

Adding to our armor, immersing ourselves in the Scriptures is not merely for comprehension but for transformation. The psalmist declared, "Your word is a lamp to my feet and a light to my path." In the chaotic blackness of trials, the Word of God provides illumination, exposing snares and revealing His sovereign guidance. Embracing God's truths fortifies our hearts against despair and fortifies our resolve to endure.

Furthermore, in the fellowship of believers lies a wellspring of mutual strength. We are not rent to endure trials in isolation; we are called into a community of grace. Encouragement from fellow pilgrims, wise counsel, and shared experiences create a bulwark of support, reminding us that we are part of a larger narrative, a tapestry woven together by our collective faith journeys.

Remembering that faith is not meant to suppress or neglect our emotions is also imperative. Lamentations have their place in the life of faith. Mourning, questioning, and yearning are human expressions God does not ignore. After all, Christ Himself wept, agonized, and petitioned God. Yet, even as we lay bare our souls in times of trial, faith whispers to us to rise once more, set our gaze on the things above, and find solace in the promise of resurrection and eternal life.

The narratives of Shadrach, Meshach, and Abednego offer a remarkable outlook on facing fiery trials. In the very flames meant to consume them, they encountered the presence of the fourth man, who was like the Son of God. Might it be that our most profound encounters with the divine are reserved for those moments when we face the fire with unwavering belief?

As we consider our trials, let us be mindful that our faith is not in the religion itself but in the One who is faithful. Like a lighthouse beacon standing firmly against the storm, God's faithfulness guides us safely to shore. Therefore, let our faith be active, not passive. Let it dance in the rain, stand firm against the wind, and look to the break of dawn with hope.

Trials have a way of stripping away the superfluous, revealing what truly matters. When faith is all, we have, we discover that faith is all we need. In the apparent weakness of our trials, the strength of our Savior becomes our anthem, for His power is perfected in our imperfections.

We understand that facing trials with faith is not a call to deny reality but to confront it with a spiritual tenacity that declares, "Even here, God is good, and His mercy endures forever." Our trials, be they great or small, serve as the canvas upon which the majesty of our God is painted in vivid strokes of grace, redemption, and hope. And through such trials, we emerge not merely survivors but overcomers by the blood of the Lamb and the word of our testimony.

The Word as Our Source of Comfort

When the gales of life menace our peace, Scripture stands as our bastion of hope—a source of solace that whispers truth amid the clamor of trials. Through its verses, one finds a dialogue with the Divine, where God's own words bring warmth to cold, weary hearts. It's in the gentle rhythm of the Psalms, the steadfast assurances in the Prophets, or the living hope declared by the Apostles that we uncover a wellspring of comfort. For isn't it written that the Word of God is living and active, cutting to the heart of our experiences, assuaging our fears, and bolstering our resolve? In moments of distress, it's neither platitudes nor mere optimism that carry us, but rather the robust promises etched in Scripture—one can't help but be cradled in its strength. Thus, let us lean into the Word, allowing the Holy Scripture to be the salve for our wounds and the light guiding us through life's inevitable storms.

Scriptures for Encouragement and Hope

In the journey of faith, moments arise when the soul thirsts for encouragement and the heart seeks solace in hope. In such times, the sacred scriptures become wells of living water, offering words that enliven the spirit and fortify the weary. These biblical passages have been a refuge throughout the ages, their inspiration undiminished by time. As the psalmist says, "God is our refuge and strength, an ever-present help in trouble" (Psalm 46:1).

The scriptures offer abundant encouragement. Consider the words of Isaiah, who provides a divine promise of strength and help, saying, "Fear not, for I am with you; be not dismayed, for I am your God; I will strengthen you, I will help you, I will uphold you with my righteous right hand" (Isaiah 41:10). In life's storms, these words are a steadfast anchor, reassuring us that we are not alone; the Almighty is invariably at our side.

Moreover, the book of Jeremiah offers a prophecy that encapsulates God's enduring love and plans for us — "For I know the plans I have for you, declares the Lord, plans for welfare and not for evil, to give you a future and a hope" (Jeremiah 29:11). This assurance provides an unshakable foundation upon which hope is built, reminding us that even during trials, God's ultimate intention is for our good.

The New Testament, too, abounds with verses that uplift the soul. In the fellowship of believers, Romans 15:4 enlightens the purpose of the scriptures, stating, "For whatever was written in former days was written for our instruction, that through endurance and the encouragement of the Scriptures, we might have hope." This serves as a reminder that scriptural wisdom is not merely historical but alive and active, intended for our endurance and upliftment.

In the letters of Paul, we find a treasure trove of encouragement. Look to Philippians 4:13, proclaiming, "I can do all things through him who strengthens me." Such a powerful declaration reinforces the belief that our capacity to overcome adversity does not spring from within ourselves but from the indwelling strength God graciously supplies.

The Psalms contribute melody to the chorus of encouragement — "The Lord is my light and my salvation; whom shall, I fear? The Lord is the stronghold of my life; of whom shall I be afraid?" (Psalm 27:1). These questions rhetorically affirm the confidence we have in God's protection and guidance.

When we face periods of loss or disappointment, the scriptures nudge us toward the hope of restoration and renewal. Lamentations 3:22-23 offer this perspective: "The steadfast love of the Lord never ceases; his mercies never come to an end; they are new every morning; great is your faithfulness." Acknowledging the inexhaustible mercy of God provides comfort that each day brings opportunities for healing and new beginnings.

Jesus Christ, the embodiment of grace and truth, also presents hope through his teachings. His words in Matthew 11:28 extend an invitation of reprieve to all, "Come to me, all who labor and are heavy laden, and I will give you rest." In this open call, Christ offers a safe harbor from the turbulence of life, providing peace that the world cannot give.

The scripture's power to encourage is on full display as we peruse the writings of John, especially in 1 John 4:4 — "He who is in you is greater than he who is in the world." This assertion encourages believers to know that the dwelling Spirit surpasses any external foe or challenge.

In this harmony of Biblical inspiration, we find a collective voice calling us to hope. There's a rich comfort found in Hebrews 6:19, which describes hope as "a sure and steadfast anchor of the soul." It's a testament to the trustworthiness of God's promises and the secure future for those anchored in faith.

Amidst life's uncertainties, 2 Corinthians 4:16-18 offers wisdom to elevate our gaze beyond the temporal, stating, "So we do not lose heart. Though our outer self wastes away, our inner self is renewed daily." These verses encourage us not to fixate on transient troubles but to look to the eternal weight of glory that awaits those who believe.

Therefore, through such sacred texts, one's faith is replenished, and the spirit is clad anew with strength. As individuals and a collective of faith, we take hold of these scriptures for encouragement and hope, allowing them to be the lamp unto our feet and the light unto our path (Psalm 119:105).

Encouragement and hope are not simply emotions or states of mind, but active pursuits prompted by solid promises of God revealed in his Word. To cling to scripture is to grasp an outstretched hand in the darkest of nights, pulling us towards the dawn of joy and peace.

Let us, therefore, immerse ourselves in the Word, drawing from it the sustenance needed for the journey. The path may be arduous and the climb steep, but with scriptural truths as our compass, we shall persevere and emerge stronger, our hearts buoyant with enduring hope and encouragement.

Pray Through Difficult Times

The Bible says, "Rejoice always, pray without ceasing, give thanks in all circumstances; for this is the will of God in Christ Jesus for you" (1 Thessalonians 5:16-17). You don't know what date and time the prayer would be most potent. Within life's unpredictable sea, there are storms we can neither foresee nor avoid. When such challenges disrupt the tranquility of our journey, we're often reminded of our vulnerability and our desperate need for a beacon of hope. The Word of God serves as a lamp unto our feet; prayer, however, is our direct line to the

Father, a means by which our souls can find solace and strength amid tumult.

In the throes of adversity, prayer often becomes a wellspring of comfort, a private dialogue between a fragile heart and a compassionate God. We're called to confidently present our requests, fears, and even our dismay before the throne of grace, knowing that we will receive mercy and find grace to help us in our time of need.

Recall the poignant words of the psalmist, who frequently found himself in peril. In his earnest pleas, he painted pictures of raw human emotion, candidly expressing his distress while anchoring his hope firmly in the steadfast love of God. His prayers remind us that while our feelings may ebb and flow, the faithfulness of our Creator remains constant.

To pray during difficult times is to exercise faith. It requires us to believe beyond what we can see, trusting that an omnipotent God is actively engaged in the intricate details of our lives. Even when the tears of struggle blur our vision, we must cling to this truth as Jacob did when he wrestled with the angel, not letting go until he received a blessing.

Yet, praying through difficulty isn't merely asking for relief. It's also about seeking understanding and peace that surpasses human wisdom. The Word of God whispers to us in these trying moments, advocating endurance and patience. The narratives of Scripture brim with stories of saints who weathered great trials, demonstrating that perseverance in prayer is often the crucible where faith is refined.

Sometimes, in our prayer journey, we discover that the purpose of our trials may not be to weaken us but to rid us of that which cannot endure eternity. As gold is tested by fire, our faith is proved genuine when laid upon the altar of affliction, a fortifying process captured profoundly within the epistles.

So, in these difficult times, let prayer be our first response, not our last resort. Cultivating a habit of turning to God amidst every tribulation builds a foundation for a responsive and resilient faith. Through continuous, earnest communication with the Almighty, we realize our dependence upon His sovereign will and perfect timing.

However, for some, the question arises of what to pray for when words fail, and the heart is heavy. In such instances, we recall the promise that the Spirit intercedes for us with groanings too deep for words. Our silent prayers, weeping, and even wordless pauses are not lost in translation; they're fully by the One who searches our hearts.

Hence, we lean not on our understanding, allowing the prayers of others to uplift us too. The joined forces of intercession strengthen the weary hearts, reminding us that while we may be hard-pressed on every side, we are not crushed; perplexed, but not in despair; persecuted, but not abandoned; struck down, but not destroyed.

Let us not forget the power of thanksgiving in our prayers as well. As we pray to Him for deliverance and guidance, we recount the manifold blessings He has already poured upon us. In fostering a spirit of gratitude, we might find joy amidst sorrow, keeping our hearts attuned to the beauty and goodness that persists around us.

In navigating through the hard seasons, our prayers might also involve a posture of listening—an openness to receiving the quiet wisdom that often follows a storm. The practice of solitude and silence before the Lord can usher in profound peace and guidance not found in the clamor of our thoughts.

As we engage in the labor of prayer, we must hold fast to the promises of Scripture. His Word is a proclamation of hope that no tribulation can separate us from His love. This assurance fuels our perseverance as we continue to pray without ceasing, confident that our cries reach the ears of a Father who is compassionate and faithful.

Therefore, let every soul afflicted by the trials of this world anchor themselves in the efficacy of prayer. Although pain may be present and the future uncertain, the power of prayer in difficult times lies in its ability to transform us, aligning our hearts with His will and reminding us that though our outer self may waste away, our inner self is being renewed daily.

In the grand tapestry of life, may our prayers be woven as threads of trust, interlaced with the enduring truth of God's Word. God's voyage through turbulent waters has passed. May we emerge with a deeper reliance on the One who calms the wind and the waves and a stronger faith that holds firm, come what may.

Chapter 7:
Sharing Grace and the Word

Upon riding the waves through the tumultuous storm of life's challenges, we find ourselves on the calm shores of purpose: to share the immeasurable grace we have been gifted and to unfurl the Word that has steadied our souls. The act of dissemination is not merely a responsibility, but a natural outpouring of a heart transformed, a life renewed.

As ambassadors of Christ, we are called to approach this privilege not with an air of superiority, but with the gentleness and reverence that signify our own receipt of grace. Constantly nourished by Scripture, our eloquence is not our own but borrowed from the divine, enabling us to share effectively without altering the purity of its truth. To witness through both grace and veracity is to walk the tightrope with a safety net below; the Spirit both guides our words and catches those we address, should they fall. Hence, let us be diligent in turning our hearts outward, ensuring that grace is not a reservoir but a river—flowing from us into the parched land of human souls searching for a drop of hope.

Spread the Gospel of Grace

As we've established our lives on the bedrock of grace, the Gospel beckons us to become bearers of this splendid truth. Spreading the Gospel of Grace isn't merely a call to evangelize, but an invitation to share the pulsating life found within the message of divine love and mercy.

It's in this sharing that our own understanding deepens, much like a fragrance that clings to the hand that distributes roses. The Gospel of Grace whispers into the recesses of weary hearts, offering rest and salvation, and we, as vessels of this Gospel, are called to pour out the same unmerited favor that we have so lavishly received.

In the midst of a world acquainted with despair, our mission is to illuminate the path with hope, articulating that salvation isn't earned by merit but is a gift for those who believe. Anchored in the assurance that Christ's work is complete, we can't help but share this uncontainable grace that has transformed our lives, thus fulfilling our role in the Great Commission, to be ambassadors of reconciliation to a fractured world.

The Great Commission

As we embark on a journey through the rivers of grace and the vast expanses of Scripture, we come upon a defining moment not only in the life of every believer but in the very mission of the Church—the Great Commission. This charge, imparted by Christ Himself, stands as a sentinel at the cusp of His ascension, beckoning all who would follow Him to a cause greater than themselves.

The command to make disciples of all nations echoes through the corridors of time, not losing vigor, and indeed, it seems to gain intensity as the years pass. It is as if each whisper of 'go therefore' multiplies and gains weight as it reverberates off the walls of human history. Within these two words lies the thrust of evangelistic endeavor—the propulsion that drives missions and the evangelization of untold millions across the globe.

To "go" is a verb that pulsates with movement and action. This is not the sedentary calling of a passive faith but the active deployment of a vibrant belief in the resurrected Christ—this call-to-action steps beyond the walls of what is comfortable into what only faith can navigate. As bearers of the Word, we go not merely in our strength but propelled by the grace that has transformed us, the grace we are commissioned to share.

Teaching, baptizing, and nurturing new believers encapsulates the passageway through which the grace individuals have hitherto experienced is passed on. In making disciples, we effectively open the floodgates for others to enter the richness of life with Christ. It is not the mere acquisition of intellectual ascent to doctrine but the cultivation of an intimate relationship with the living Word, the Sower of all truth.

Another aspect of the Great Commission addresses the very scope of the mission—' all nations.' Here, diversity and the valorization of every culture come to the fore. Our calling is to every tribe, language, and people group. The inclusivity of the gospel becomes apparent through this mandate; no one is beyond the reach of God's grace nor the embrace of His Word.

Undergirding the command to make disciples is the assurance of Christ's perpetual presence—' I am with you always, to the end of the age.' The visibility of the Savior might have been withdrawn from our physical sight, yet His nearness is assured to us in ways more profound than our senses can detect. He who commands us also commits to journey alongside us every step of the way. His permanent availability to the believer bestows courage, wisdom, and strength for the task at hand.

A pivotal element often overlooked is the heart's posture of the one who commissions. Jesus, in whom the fullness of grace and truth dwelt bodily, transmitted the baton with the same grace that characterized His earthly ministry. Thus, while grounded in truth, our methodology must equally be saturated with His grace. We must mirror the grace we preach, becoming living epistles of the Word we carry.

The Great Commission calls for a particular transformation—a metamorphosis in personal life and collective ecclesiastical expression. We are to be transformed so that we may be agents of transformation, stewards of a heavenly inheritance to be thoroughly enjoyed and freely bestowed. In its essence, the Commission is an invitation to participate in the divine nature through the onward propagation of the gospel.

Being witnesses unto Christ is not a mere sidebar in the Christian life but is intrinsic to our identity in Him. In His words, 'You will be my witnesses...' is the mandate. It foretells a life so interwoven with His that our own stories become indistinguishable from the grand narrative of redemption. We are the mosaics through which His story is told, a story that finds its strength in our weaknesses, its eloquence in our stumbles, and its appeal in our diversity.

The grace encountered through our fledgling faith is the same grace we encourage others to embrace. As vessels of this grace, our transformation validates the message we propagate. The word 'hypocrite' finds no harbor in the heart of one who lives out the Word authentically, ensuring that the grace we teach is the grace we live.

Finally, there is an imperative to return to the source—the Word of God continually. In the Bible, we find the descriptions of Christ's life and teachings that we are to model and relay; we find the energy for our Commission. The Word is both our map and our compass on this mission. Without it, we veer off course; with it, we navigate the tumultuous seas of human existence. The Great Commission, anchored in the Word, becomes not merely an earthly strategy but a spiritual encounter with eternal ramifications.

As we labor in this calling, we lean heavily upon the grace that saves and sends. This grace has marked us, equipped us, and will sustain us as we each play our part in the divine symphony of redemption. We are woven into the rich tapestry of God's redemptive plan, and the Great Commission is our thread—bold and unbreakable—sewing us into the fabric of a world awaiting the hope found in Christ alone.

Therefore, embarking on the endeavor of the Great Commission is not to set out on a foolhardy quest but to walk in obedience to a high and heavenly call. In this humbling yet exalting task, we find our purpose and greatest joy, for in obediently stepping out, we discover the intimate presence of Christ, the depth of His grace, and the transformative power of His Word.

In conclusion, let us embrace the Great Commission with sincere hearts and diligent steps, with our hearts firmly rooted in grace and our hands skillfully handling the Word of truth. Herein lies our calling and our charge—to go, make disciples, teach, and baptize, all the while bearing witness to the One who has called us out of darkness into His marvelous light.

Being Ambassadors of Christ

As we delve further into the exploration of God's grace and the significance of His Word in our lives, one cannot overlook the profound responsibility that comes with such divine understanding. Having been recipients of such unmerited favor and spiritual guidance, we stand as representatives, as ambassadors of Christ in a world that is often unaware of or resistant to the message of His love and truth. An ambassador is charged with representing the interests and character of the one who sent them, embodying their values, and conveying their message with clarity and conviction.

In biblical times, the role of an ambassador was crucial. They spoke on behalf of kings and kingdoms, and the weight of their words could mean peace or war. Today, as followers of Jesus, we are called to be ambassadors of the Kingdom of Heaven. This calling is as potent and necessary as it was in the days of the apostles. To be Christ's representative means to live lives infused with His grace so others may know Him through us.

Our speech and actions must reflect the One we serve. Our conversations, filled with grace, should be seasoned with the salt of wisdom so we might know how to answer everyone. Just as a skilled ambassador learns the languages and customs of the territories in which they operate, so must we understand the people and culture we are called to reach. This requires sensitivity, an open heart, and listening before speaking.

Furthermore, an ambassador operates with authority. When we speak the truths of scripture and proclaim the gospel, we are not presenting our ideas but those of our Lord. And with the authority given to us by Christ comes the assurance that the power of the Kingdom of Heaven fully backs us. In this power, we stand against injustice, offer hope to the broken, and spread the love of God liberally, as we have freely received.

As ambassadors of Christ, we are not promised a path without challenges. Indeed, there will be opposition, misunderstandings, and, sometimes, outright rejection of our message. Yet, through these trials, our ambassadorship is refined, and our dependence on God's grace is deepened. The strength we exhibit in the face of adversity becomes a testimony that speaks volumes to the steadfastness of God's presence in our lives.

Love is the badge of our office. The love we show is not mere human affection but a supernatural fruit of the Spirit dwelling within us. This love will cause us to see the needs of others and move us to action. It is a love that forgives endlessly, extends mercy generously, and cares deeply for the welfare of others—mirroring the love Christ has shown us.

However, being ambassadors of Christ does not mean we are perfect emissaries. We are flawed vessels, but this human imperfection is where God's power is perfected. Our weaknesses are conduits for His strength, and His grace is sufficient for us. When we stumble, we can receive forgiveness and learn to forgive ourselves and others with grace-inspired compassion.

Patience is another virtue intrinsic to our ambassadorial role. The transformation of hearts and minds is not instantaneous. Therefore, we must be patient as we share God's Word and navigate the journey with those who are grappling with the truths we present. Patience also means enduring through seasons of waiting—waiting for hearts to soften and change and for God's timing in our lives and ministries.

An ambassador must also be a skilled communicator, understanding what to say and how to say it. We must ensure that our communication is bridge-building, not barrier-forming, that it opens doors rather than closes them. Each interaction is an opportunity to demonstrate the character of the King we serve—full of grace and truth.

Maintaining a lifestyle of worship is another essential aspect of our ambassadorship. Worship aligns our hearts with God's; through it, we declare His worth, sovereignty, and majesty. As we live in continuous adoration, others are drawn into the presence of God, even those who might never step foot in a church.

Engaging in the ministry of reconciliation is a fundamental task for an ambassador of Christ. This is the heart of the gospel—to restore the relationship between God and man. In our pursuit of peace and reconciliation, we mirror the reconciling work of Christ, inviting others into restored relationships with God and one another.

Finally, the journey of being an ambassador of Christ means that we are constantly learning and growing in our faith. This endeavor has neither a pinnacle nor a plateau; it is a continuous progression towards Christlikeness. This growth involves regular immersion in scripture, allowing the living Word to shape our thoughts, guide our actions, and reinforce our calling.

In this sacred position, we must also embody humility. An ambassador does not seek their glory but aims to amplify the message and the sender. Our service is a reflection of the selflessness of Christ, who came not to be served but to serve and to give His life as a ransom for many.

While being an ambassador for Christ is a high calling, it comes with profound support – the indwelling of the Holy Spirit. We are not left to our own devices; we have a Counselor, a Guide, and an Advocate who leads us and empowers us for every good work. We can rest in this assurance as we embody our ambassadorial role.

In summary, being ambassadors of Christ is a multifaceted and glorious calling. As we press on in this high calling, let us hold fast to the grace that saves us, the Word that guides us, and the Spirit that empowers us. May we represent our King with the nobility, love, and faithfulness He deserves so that the world may know the One we are privileged to serve through our lives.

Equipped by the Word

As disciples of Christ, we are graced with the charge to share His love and truth with the world around us. Being well-equipped by the Word is, therefore, an imperative that echoes through our calling. Immersion in Scripture not only solidifies our understanding but also ignites the passion to impart the richness of God's promises to others. We must become adept at wielding Scripture, not as a weapon forged for judgment, but as a balm for world-weary souls longing to be revived by the eternal hope we have tethered our lives to.

Through disciplined study, guided application, and heartfelt prayer, the very verses that have transformed our lives can become vessels of grace in the lives of those we meet. Anchored in the Word, our conversations can naturally overflow with scriptural wisdom, making us ready in season and out of season to offer a reason for the joy that lives within us – with gentleness and respect, as stewards of God's unshakeable truth.

Sharing Scripture Effectively

As we journey through life's tapestry, woven with threads of grace and guided by the Word, we come to the pivotal task of sharing these sacred texts. This endeavor, far from being a mere recitation of verses, transcends into an art—sharing scripture with effectiveness so that it plants seeds of truth and faith in the hearts of listeners.

The sacred act of sharing scripture stretches beyond our understanding; it is an intricate interplay of the Divine and the human heart. Let us immerse ourselves in prayer before we embark on this noble quest. We seek discernment, wisdom, and an outpouring of love so that our words might become vessels of the Holy Spirit rather than mere echoes of human thought.

Understanding context is crucial to sharing effectively. As we approach scripture, let us be sensitive to the reality that these words were penned in a time far removed from our own. Therefore, endeavor to bridge the gap between the ancient and the contemporary so that the Word speaks as vibrantly today as it did to those who first heard its voice.

Clarity and simplicity pave the way for comprehension. Approach the sharing of scripture with the intent to make plain its truths. Jesus Himself spoke in parables—stories that resonated with the commoner yet were replete with heavenly wisdom. Strive to find relatable stories to illuminate the truths of scripture for those you address.

It's essential that sharing scripture isn't an exercise in intellectualism. It must deeply connect with everyday life. It's not enough to share the Word; we must show how it breathes life into every moment of our existence. How does this verse, passage, and story intersect with your life, my life, our triumphs, and our struggles?

Encounter those you share with where they are. Every heart is tilling its soil, grappling with unique challenges and aspirations. Speak the Word in a manner that recognizes and respects this individual journey. To effectively share scripture, one must listen intently, engage with genuine interest, and respond with passages that speak to the individual's condition.

Do not be discouraged if the message you share falls on arid ground. Remember, the Word of God is living and powerful, and even the smallest seed, sown in faith, can burgeon into a bountiful harvest in due season. Our charge is but to scatter the seed; it is God who lovingly tends to its growth.

Let us not forget the significance of a life lived as a testament to our shared scriptures. Our actions often speak louder than our words. A compassionate act can illuminate a verse far brighter than the most eloquent discourse, just as a life of integrity can provide the fertile ground for the seeds of God's Word to flourish.

There are moments when sharing the scriptures may require courage. Speaking truth can stir resistance, perhaps even hostility. Here, too, we look to scripture for courage, remembering that the prophets and apostles were no strangers to adversity. Stand firm, then, and let your speech always be seasoned with grace so you may know how to answer each person.

Sharing scripture demands patience; there is profound wisdom in understanding the pace of the Spirit's work in a person's heart. Pressing too hard or too soon can be counterproductive. Instead, allow space and time in your sharing so that the Holy Spirit might gently, yet powerfully, move upon the listener's heart.

Recalling that our ultimate aim is not to win arguments but to win souls, we must be ever so careful to avoid debates that inflate our egos. The Word we share is not our own; we are mere messengers of the King. Therefore, let us speak with the humility befitting servants of the Most High.

Intercession is our hidden strength when sharing scripture. While we may converse with humans, it is primarily a spiritual endeavor. Interceding for those we share with invites God's power and presence into their lives, opening doors for the transformative work of the Word.

To share scripture effectively is to weave it seamlessly into the conversations of life, to find opportune moments, and to recognize them as divinely appointed. A word aptly spoken, a scripture shared in due season, how good it is — like apples of gold in settings of silver.

Finally, we must trust. Trust in the power of the Word to penetrate hearts and transform lives. Trust in the Spirit's guidance as we share. Trust that the seeds we plant are never in vain. As we share scripture, we embark on the holy ground of divine encounter—an encounter that could alter the course of life for eternity.

Therefore, as we find ourselves equipped and inspired to share God's Word, let us engage this task with the reverence it deserves. Let us intercede, listen, communicate, and live so that those we minister may not just hear words but encounter the living Word through the grace-filled ministry of our sharing.

Witnessing through Grace and Truth is not merely a call to speak but an invitation to live authentically amid a fractured world. As we've explored the boundless reaches of grace and delved into the profound depths of Scripture, we now come to the palpable intersection of theory and action. For it's in the daily endeavors, spurred on by our foundational beliefs, that we genuinely testify to the life-changing power of the divine narrative we hold dear.

It's essential to grasp that witnessing through grace and truth isn't a balancing act, with grace on one side and truth on the other. No, both qualities' harmonious and simultaneous expression illuminates Christ in us. One can't help but recall John's Gospel, where the Word-made flesh is said to be full of grace and truth. We seek to emulate this same fullness in our encounters with others.

To witness through grace is to extend the same unmerited favor we have received. It's a kindness that doesn't wait for the other to be deserving but rushes out to meet them in their need. It reflects a heart changed by divine mercy, a heart that echoes the Father's generosities. This form of grace in our witness is not indicative of weakness; instead, it stands as a testament to the strength given to us, a strength that allows us to love unconditionally.

In parallel, witnessing through truth is to remain anchored to the Word in every situation. It's the courage to uphold God's standards, to speak with conviction, and to let one's life be a genuine representation of biblical principles. Far from being rigid, the commitment to truth reflects the steadfastness of God's promises and the reliability of His commandments as the foundation of life.

Now, you may ponder, how do we effectively embody both without compromising one for the sake of the other? Witnessing through grace and truth starts by immersing oneself in loving introspection and study of the Scriptures. Our understanding of grace and truth deepens when we diligently tune to the Spirit's guidance through the sacred text. Knowledge is vital, but so is sensitivity to the Spirit's leading.

Practically, our witness is shaped not only by what we say but predominantly through how we live. Our actions often speak with greater volume than our words. It's in extending a helping hand to people in need, forgiving the erring, and showing patience in affliction that we display the grace we speak of. Similarly, our adherence to truth is seen when we choose integrity over convenience, align our choices with our convictions, and stand firm in faith despite opposition.

However, let us not fall into the trap of believing we can witness effectively through our power. By the Spirit's work within us, we are enabled to live out this dual call. Such divine empowering gives us the wisdom to know when to speak up, be silent, offer mercy, and stand firm.

It's critical to recognize that our audience—those we are called to witness—are individuals with unique experiences and backgrounds. Each person requires a tailored approach, a message wrapped in compassion and imbued with objective truth. We can't afford to present half-measures of either grace or truth, for one without the other is an incomplete picture of the Gospel we profess.

In this delicate task, confound not the role of a peacemaker with that of a pleaser. To witness with grace and truth may involve difficult conversations and moments of uncomfortable clarity. Here, we should strive to be gracious in approach but uncompromising in the truth we share.

Moreover, while we carry this treasure in earthen vessels, let's be gentle with ourselves. We are bound to fumble, to falter in our attempts to witness rightly. Yet, it is in these stumblings that grace again covers us, and truth reminds us that we are but human, dependent on the One who is perfect. Perseverance is critical; ours is not a one-time act of witness but a sustained life of testimony.

As we wrap ourselves in these divine concepts, let's embrace the diverse platforms for witnessing. Our witness can and should be manifold through the spoken Word, the written letter, acts of service, and the ubiquity of digital expressions. Not limited to pulpit or podium, grace, and truth find their way into workplaces, schools, homes, and beyond.

Remember, the power of listening is an often-overlooked aspect of witnessing. In listening, we offer dignity to the speaker, reflecting God's regard for us. Authentic listening can open the door to hearts closed tight by hurt or misunderstanding and lay the groundwork for seeds of grace and truth to take root.

With clear eyes fixed on Jesus, we set out, know, and wing full well the weight of such a calling. In our relational world, we are emissaries of the King, and every interaction is an opportunity to showcase His magnificence. It's a daunting yet thrilling charge that we carry not in the strength of our flesh but propelled by Spirit and tethered by grace and truth.

In conclusion, let us then be mindful of this great responsibility. Let's hold fast to what we have learned about grace and truth, striving to apply it in all facets of life. Let's cherish this precious calling and approach our witness with humility, knowing that the Lord works to will and act according to His good pleasure. Our task is to walk in step with Him, living as beacons of grace and truth amidst the shadows of our time.

Chapter 8:
Living a Life Anchored in the
Word and Sponsored by Grace

As the journey through life's ebbs and flows continues, the task at hand is not merely surviving the torrents but flourishing within them. This way of life, anchored unwaveringly in the Word and sponsored by the unending resources of God's grace, becomes more than a mere existential stance; it grows to be the very essence of our being. Anchored believers find themselves not tossed about by the vicissitudes of life but rather grounded in a reality that holds firm even amid the tumult.

It's in the transformative power of this divine anchor that wisdom and peace are found and the sweet sovereign grace acts as an unceasing sponsor to this spiritual voyage. Embracing such a saturated life necessitates a heart that not only receives grace but also permits it to overflow into every interaction, decision, and thought. With the Scriptures as the rudder guiding through tempests and doldrums alike, this life becomes a testament to perseverance—and it's in this steadfastness the foundation of faith is both visible and effective. The call to abide is not passive but echoes strongly through the ages, urging all to remain in Christ, who is the Word incarnate, and in the grace, He so lavishly pours out, promising more than mere existence, promising an abundant life that overflows with joy, peace, and unfettered hope.

The Transformative Journey

As we wade deeper into the waters of spiritual understanding, the transformative journey becomes starkly apparent, marked by the ripples of grace and the solid ground of the Word beneath our feet. This path of transformation weaves through the everyday fabric of our lives, challenging us to reflect upon our personal growth, stripping us of pride, and humbling our hearts before the majesty of God's gracious design.

It's about perseverance in faith, ever pressing onward, even when storms gather, and the way seems obscured. Such a journey isn't solely about reaching a destination, but rather about the ongoing process of becoming—immersing ourselves in the sanctifying flow of divine favor, while being rooted ever more firmly in the bedrock of Scripture. Embracing this journey, we discover the true essence of living a life sponsored by God's grace—a dynamic odyssey that reshapes us from within, securing our steps and propelling us toward His ultimate call.

Reflect on Personal Growth

As we explore growth, it is pivotal to recognize that it is not merely an acquisition of knowledge but a transformation of the heart, mind, and soul. This growth is intertwined with grace and cannot be separated from the sacred Word that guides us. Our journey thus far has shed light on the foundations of faith, the significance of grace, and the roles both play in transformation, relationships, and navigating life's trials. Now, we turn inward to reflect on personal growth through the mirror of grace.

Personal growth is a testament to a faith nourished by divine grace. It echoes through the corridors of a believer's life, whispering reminders of where they've been and how far they've come. In the quiet recesses of the heart, one discovers the incremental changes shaped by daily encounters with Scripture and the subtle workings of grace. Each verse internalized, each prayer whispered, contributes to a soul's steady progression toward the likeness of Christ.

Consider for a moment the parable of the Sower. Like seeds scattered across various soils, the Word of God falls upon our hearts in diverse conditions. The growth we observe in ourselves hinges on how deeply we allow these seeds to take root. Rocky ground may have impeded us initially, or thorns of worldly concern may have threatened to choke our budding faith. Yet, by continually seeking God's grace and meditating on His Word, the once dure ground becomes fertile, yielding a harvest of spiritual maturity.

The metrics of personal growth in a believer's life are often subtle: patience in tribulation, kindness in adversity, and love in the face of hostility. Such traits don't bloom overnight but are cultivated through seasons of reliance on grace and constant communion with the Word. In the silent victory over a long-held grudge or the gentle response to provocation, one measures the distance traveled on this transformative journey.

The Scriptures equip us for every good work, guiding us towards growth in holiness and godliness. As we apply the Word to our lives, we find ourselves increasingly uncomfortable with actions and attitudes that fall short of the glory of God. Personal growth becomes visible in our repentance and the deliberate striving away from sin. Consequently, we become living testimonies of the sanctifying power of grace.

Embracing discipline is also part of reflecting on personal growth. Discipline in study, prayer, and communion with God through His Word is instrumental to transformation. It's often in the daily commitment to these spiritual disciplines that we find incremental changes accumulating, shaping us closer to the divine calling upon our lives. Self-control, godliness, and steadfastness are born in disciplined practice.

Engaging with the community of believers is also reflective of personal growth. As we immerse ourselves in the body of Christ, we learn humility, service, and the value of supportive relationships. This growth is evident as we find ourselves more inclined to forgive, quicker to serve, and eager to build up others in their faith—mirroring the grace that we have received.

Reflecting on personal growth in the storms of life means recognizing how our responses have transformed. The challenges that once may have shaken our foundations now become occasions to demonstrate our anchor in God's promises. Through grace, we become individuals who, even when buffeted by the winds of trial, remain steadfast in faith, anchored by the Word.

It is also in moments of failure and weakness that personal growth becomes apparent. When we fall, grace is at hand not only to forgive but also to teach us. Reflecting on past mistakes through the lens of Scripture inspires sober self-examination and ignites determination to grow from each experience. Growth is measured not by never falling but by rising each time we do with increased strength and wisdom granted by grace.

Mindful witnessing of God's hand in our lives prompts gratitude, another marker of personal growth. As we progress in our faith journey, observing grace in the minutest details of daily life cultivates a heart of gratitude. This gratitude spills over into our language, demeanor, and actions, affecting every sphere of our existence with positivity and peace.

Fruitfulness in ministry is a further reflection of growth. As we mature, our capacity to serve and impact others for Christ expands. Our spiritual gifts are honed and exercised with greater efficacy in teaching, encouragement, hospitality, or leadership. The realization that we're conduits of grace to the world is both humbling and exhilarating, propelling us into more outstanding works for the Kingdom.

Personal growth in the context of eternity means keeping our lives anchored in the lasting rather than the fleeting. The Scriptures refocus our perspective, allowing us to see beyond the temporal. Our values, goals, and dreams align more with God's eternal purposes, demonstrating a profound and transformative shift in our priorities and actions.

This reflective journey leads us to acknowledge grace's role in enabling perseverance. It is grace that buoys our faith during periods of waiting and uncertainty. Our growth narrative is punctuated by instances where we could've given up but instead chose to cling to the assurances found in God's Word. Thus, perseverance is both a product and a sign of maturation in faith.

In times of solitude and meditation, personal growth whispers its presence. In the serenity of one's quiet time with the Lord, insights gleaned from Scripture crystallize into life-changing convictions. The transformation we undergo often catches its most profound glimpses when we are alone with God, allowing His Spirit to work within us, guiding us gently towards greater Christlikeness.

Lastly, growth is seen in our capacity to love. The Word of God, alive and active, instructs us to love God and our neighbor unequivocally. As the Holy Spirit works within us, our ability to extend love broadens, often pushing past human limitations. A growing love for God and His creation indicates that we are moving forward, ever becoming the person God intends us to be. In the interplay of grace and the Word, personal growth is about becoming less of ourselves and more of Him—manifesting the nature of Christ in a world in dire need of His touch.

Persevere in Faith

As we continue on this transformative journey, it becomes evident that perseverance in faith is not a casual endeavor. Much like a tree driving its roots deep into the earth to withstand the force of a storm, we must ground ourselves deeply in faith to navigate the complexities of life. But what does it mean to persevere in faith? To persevere means to continue steadfastly or determinedly despite difficulties or discouragement.

First, let's recall that faith is described in Hebrews as the substance of things hoped for, the evidence of things not seen. This assurance isn't a passive acceptance but an active pursuit involving our will, mind, and emotions, engaged and aligned towards God's promises. Perseverance is how this pursuit maintains its momentum through high seas and calm waters.

Let us examine the life of Abraham, who is often called the Father of Faith. He was called to leave everything familiar and venture into the unknown based on God's promises. His journey was not without moments of doubt or failure, but his narrative highlights the beauty of steadfast trust in God's Word. Persevering faith involves holding to promises even when the circumstances surrounding us seem to deny their possibility.

One might ask, how do we muster such persistence? James reminds us that perseverance must finish its work so that we may be mature and complete, not lacking anything. It's forged in the fires of trials and challenges; to persevere, we must face and navigate hardships, using them as tools to strengthen our faith. It is not the absence of adversity that fortifies us but our response to it, underpinned by the knowledge of God's grace and truth.

In the realm of perseverance, prayer becomes our indispensable ally. When Paul speaks of praying without ceasing, he isn't advocating for a non-stop verbal exercise but rather a heart constantly attuned to and reliant upon God's presence. Our prayers are like a river that, though it may change in volume and pace, continuously flows toward the expanse of God's will.

Similarly, the role of community in the concept of perseverance cannot be overstated. Galatians encourages us to carry each other's burdens and, in doing so, fulfill the law of Christ. The walk of faith was never meant to be a solitary endeavor. Our brothers and sisters provide strength, encouragement, and a tangible expression of God's grace as we face various trials.

Furthermore, the Scriptures offer us numerous reassurances that we do not persevere in our strength. Isaiah beautifully portrays God giving power to the faint and increasing the strength of those with no might. Our perseverance is amplified and sustained by relying on the Lord.

Meditating on the Word is essential in developing a heart of perseverance. As we digest the truth of Scripture, our minds are renewed, and our perspectives are aligned with God's. David's Psalms are rich with expressions of unwavering trust in God amidst affliction, serving as a model of faithfulness and as a source of comfort and encouragement for us.

Jesus Himself exemplifies perfect perseverance. Hebrews describes Him as the author and finisher of our faith, who for the joy set before Him endured the cross, scorning its shame. Here, we see the ultimate picture of perseverance—bearing the present pain for the father's promised future joy.

While Jesus endured the cross with the joy of the future in mind, it's essential to live with preparedness for the reality that some promises we cling to may only be fulfilled in eternity. This knowledge should not diminish our commitment but rather strengthen it, knowing that our labor in the Lord is not in vain.

The art of patience is cultivated within the realms of waiting. Scripture frequently admonishes the faithful to wait on the Lord—a posture that signifies hope and expectation. Our perseverance is often tested in these waiting periods, but it's also where we can experience profound spiritual growth.

Perseverance is evidenced when we look at martyrs and missionaries who faced insurmountable odds. They pressed on, not because they were immune to fear or suffering, but because they were convinced of the reality and power of the unseen kingdom. They lived out the call to endure everything for the elect's sake.

What then of the moments when we fall short, when our flesh seems too weak, and perseverance appears beyond our grasp? Here, we must recall that grace is at the core of our journey. It is by grace that we're saved through faith—and this grace is the same that empowers us to stand when we could easily fall.

In practical terms, establishing routines that align with our faith walk can help sustain our perseverance. Regular worship, engagement in service, and devout study of the Word keep the flame of faith actively burning within us. These practices become part of our spiritual armor against complacency and despair.

In the end, persevering in faith is not about never faltering but rising each time we stumble, leaning ever more into the grace that upholds us. We take heart in knowing that there is a crown of righteousness laid up for all who have loved His appearance, who endure to the end by faith. This reward, both now and in the life to come, is sustained by perseverance born from our unfailing trust in God's immovable Word and unchanging character.

The Call to Abide

In the journey of faith, abiding isn't merely a suggestion; it's a heartfelt invitation to entwine one's soul with the divine truths of Scripture, to dwell richly in the vastness of God's grace. To abide is to linger in His presence, to forge a life so deeply rooted in His Word that we can't help but reflect His love in every word, decision, and deed.

The promise of an abundant life becomes attainable as we wholeheartedly embrace this call, surrendering our wandering hearts to the steady pulse of the Spirit's guidance. It's in this sacred act of dwelling that we uncover the strength to face life's tempests, finding our mooring not in the transient, but in the eternal embrace of the Word and grace.

Remaining in God's Word and Grace is an anchorage for the soul, steadfast and unmovable, amidst the ebbs and flows of worldly trials. Embedding oneself in the divine tapestry that is Scripture and embracing the profound mystery of grace offered without merit presents a reality reoriented towards heavenly precepts. To persist within this sanctuary, one must adopt continual communion with the divine Word and a tenacious grasping of grace.

As a tree extends its roots deep into the earth to find water and nourishment, one's roots in God's Word should push ever deeper. It is not by a singular act that such growth is achieved; it entails daily discipline. Reading, meditating, and applying Scripture requires scheduled and spontaneous moments where the holy text interrupts the mundane rhythms of life. By these actions, the Word becomes engrafted into one's very being.

Grace is not a once-received gift neatly packaged, set upon a shelf, and admired from a distance. It is living, breathing, and productive, requiring an active response. To abide in grace, one must likewise embrace humility, recognizing the need for divine help and a dependence beyond human capability or merit. Acknowledging one's shortcomings drives one closer to the heart of Jesus, where grace abounds.

Regular introspection guided by the mirror of the Word illuminates the areas in one's life where grace is desperately needed. Revealing blemishes and beauty, it compels transformation—not through the sheer force of human will but through the enlivening power of the Spirit that accompanies grace. This transformation is sought in prayer, not merely as a ritual but as a dynamic dialogue with the Divine.

While drinking deeply from the well of the Word, one finds themselves immersed in a relationship. It is more than scholarship; it is a sacred dance with Truth transcending the printed page. Likewise, grace reaches beyond the abstract; it manifests in relationships, in the forgiveness offered and received, in the sacrifice mirrored after the very heart of God.

The practice of self-denial, a concept much aligned with grace, aligns one's desires with the will of God outlined in Scripture. Fasting, serving others, and sacrificial giving facilitate a release from worldly attachments, allowing God's Word and grace to fill the vacated chambers of the heart.

Moments of doubt and perplexity can assail the most devout of believers. In such times, the remembered and hidden Word sown in one's heart resurfaces as an anchor. Coupled with grace, it becomes evident that God's presence remains even in the shadowed valleys.

Through persistence in faith, one finds His grace is sufficient, and His Word is a steady guide.

A faith community acts as soil where one's roots can entwine, gaining strength from collective worship and shared stories of grace. Bearing one another's burdens, exhorting, and encouraging through Scripture, the believers find their unity in the Word and grace they hold dear.

In times of joy, God's Word offers songs of praise and verses of exultation that lift the Spirit in thankfulness. However, grace teaches that every situation, whether fraught with pain or filled with blessings, is an opportunity to experience God's proximity and provident care. One learns to be content through the inward fortitude supplied by the Spirit.

Action and reflection form a rhythm; grace and the Word necessitate both. In action, arms are stretched out towards those in need; lips speak Truth and love, and feet walk paths of righteousness guided by Biblical directives. In reflection, the soul retreats into the silent embrace of God, listens for the whisperings of the Spirit, and cherishes the sufficiency of grace.

As a life anchored in the Word and sponsored by grace endures, it becomes a beacon to the lost, a testament to God's unfailing love. The Scripture-laden soul guides others to the Truth, not through forcible argument but by the compelling narrative of a life visibly transformed by the gentleness and power of grace.

The call to abide in Jesus, as He abides in the Father, embodies the essence of this remaining. Abiding isn't merely coexisting; it intertwines will, purpose, and Spirit with the divine. The Word incarnate, Jesus, models this abiding — His actions imbued with the Father's love and grace, His every Word steeped in the authority and comfort of Scripture.

An abiding presence in God's Word and grace shapes perceptions, reorients priorities, and calibrates desires to heavenly aspirations. Earthly ambitions are tempered and reshaped into a longing for His kingdom, a pursuit of His righteousness, and a passion for His glory. This presence permeates one's entire being and infuses every pursuit with eternal significance.

As this season of reflection draws toward its conclusion, may the vision to abide in His Word and grace never wane. May the faithful, strengthened by the Spirit, persevere in their dedication to the disciplines of grace and the diligent study of the Word, knowing that they embark on a daily journey that draws them ever closer to the likeness of Christ.

Thus, to remain in God's Word and grace is to experience perpetual renewal, an endless season of growth marked by divine empowerment and unparalleled peace. In this divine abode, the believer discovers the fullness of life, a resounding echo of eternity's call, and the sweet assurance of the Savior's presence—for to abide in His Word and grace is to be anchored in the very heart of God.

The Promise of Abundant Life emerges as the culminating assurance for those who have journeyed through the teachings and transformative power of grace and the Word. In this sacred promise, we find the essence of a life genuinely anchored in spiritual depth and endless sufficiency. As we delve into this promise, we must understand that it extends beyond mere material prosperity or an untroubled existence; instead, it points to a richness of soul, an enduring peace, and an unshakeable joy that throbs at the very heart of our communion with the Divine.

To apprehend this promise fully, one must recognize the nature of abundance in a spiritual frame. This abundance manifests as an overflow of that which is eternal and incorruptible - qualities such as love, hope, peace, and faith. These are the treasures stored up in the heavens where neither moth nor rust can destroy, far outlasting the transient allure of worldly wealth and transient triumphs.

Abundant life finds its roots in the Word, which feeds and guides the seeker. Within the sacred text, one discovers the principles to navigate life's complex landscapes and the assurance of God's perpetual presence. The Word does not just inform; it transforms, casting a vision for a robust, purposeful life teeming with heavenly possibilities.

Consider grace as the divine sponsor of this life, a ceaseless river that nourishes and brings forth growth even in desert places. When grace is understood and embraced, it fosters a sense of worth and courage that is not subject to the oscillations of external conditions. Indeed, grace is the foundation upon which the promise of abundant life is built.

Abundant life in grace means living in freedom—a freedom that arises from forgiveness, the relinquishment of the bondage of sin and guilt. This liberation does not come from our futile attempts at self-improvement but from accepting the gift of grace itself. When one's identity is anchored in Christ, the chains that once ensnared are broken, and life blossoms in liberation.

Furthermore, the promise of abundance touches our relationships. As we're transformed by grace, our interactions are marked by an effervescent loving-kindness that mirrors the heavenly standard. Through our relationships, the abundant life radiates and touches others, prompting a ripple effect of grace beyond individual experience.

The abundant life also entails resilience in the face of life's storms. When storms assail, those anchored in the Word and sponsored by grace find an unwavering hope and strength that the world cannot give nor take away. It's within this stronghold that safety and peace are found, even when circumstances might suggest otherwise.

Moreover, abundant life beckons us to share the tales of grace and the truths of the Word with others. Evangelism and discipleship become not a duty but a delight, an outflow of life within us, yearning to reach others with the same hope we've been granted.

In the community, abundant life flourishes. It is not a solitary journey but one enriched by the companionship of fellow believers. In the tapestry of the body of Christ, each thread retains unique value, collectively displaying the beauty of a life interwoven by grace and truth.

Service and ministry are also integral aspects of abundant life. Trustworthy service is not a cumbersome burden but an expression of the overflow of abundance within us. When we serve from the position of grace, we discover our spiritual gifts and the joy of aligning our actions with the Divine purpose.

The discipline of gratitude is another facet of abundant life. A grateful heart recognizes the fingerprints of grace in everyday moments, constantly elevating our perspective from the temporal to the eternal. By acknowledging the countless ways grace manifests, thankfulness becomes the melody of our existence.

Regarding leadership, the abundant life directs us to lead with wisdom gleaned from the Word and humility rooted in the knowledge of grace. Such leadership is characterized by servant-heartedness, always looking to the ultimate example set by Christ himself.

As we shift our gaze towards the horizon of eternity, the promise of abundant life acquires its ultimate dimension. This perspective instructs us to live today with the future in mind, ensuring that our temporal days echo with the weight of eternal worth and significance.

Testimony is our battle cry and proof of the abundant life at work within us. In sharing our stories, we celebrate the victories won through grace and the transformations wrought by the Word. These narratives inspire and encourage, inviting others to taste the richness of life promised by our Creator.

The abundant life is thus a panoramic vista of spiritual wealth and depth, characterized by inner contentment, strength in weakness, overflow of grace, and the unfading glories that await. As we live anchored in the Word and sponsored by grace, we anticipate and participate in the abundant life promised to us—one that begins here and stretches into eternity.

Chapter 9:
Embracing Community through Grace

As we transition from the individual transformation by grace to the broader scope of its influence, it's crucial to recognize the potent role grace plays in fostering community. To embrace one another within the bonds of unity and peace is to act as living vessels of grace, extending the same unconditional love we've received. It's within this close-knit fellowship that believers encourage, edify, and uplift one another, each person a thread woven into a tapestry of shared faith.

Building a supportive network isn't just about finding a tribe; it's a conscious act of knitting our lives together so that when one falters, the others can bear them up. Encouraging each other in faith becomes the natural outflow of lives transformed by grace, a resonance that amplifies the voice of the Divine in a chorus of shared stories, struggles, and victories. Here, in the embrace of this celestial community, grace finds its most profound expression—as the love of God in action through hearts and hands unified.

Build a Supportive Network

In pursuing a life graced by God's unfailing love, believers must recognize the importance of community. The tapestry of faith is not merely woven by solitary threads of individual believers but is strengthened significantly through the bonds of a supportive network. This community is a shelter for the soul, where we learn the rhythms of grace and mercy in concert with others. In these relations, the abstract becomes tangible, where the Word's teachings on love and support find their fullest expression.

Fostering a robust spiritual network involves more than passive attendance at weekly services. It's a concerted effort to delve into meaningful relationships with those around us. Just as the early Church in the Acts of the Apostles shared their lives, so too must followers of Christ today endeavor to connect genuinely and sincerely, providing a context where believers can both offer and receive support.

Understanding that our faith journey is communal allows us to see the value in each member's unique gifts and experiences. In the book of Romans, Paul speaks to the Church's diverse talents, which are meant not just for personal improvement but for the upbuilding of the body of Christ. Indeed, within the collective, the individual is edified, corrected, and encouraged—a cycle that requires a willingness to be vulnerable and accountable.

Authentic relationships require time to nurture. Regular fellowship with a small group or a few trusted believers allows one to regularly learn from one another, pray together, and carry one another's burdens. In Galatians, we're reminded to bear one another's burdens and fulfill Christ's law. This mutuality is the hallmark of a supportive network and can't be rushed.

Creating such a network also means being proactive in reaching out—making the phone call, sending the message, or offering to meet up. As we gravitate toward others, we must remain rooted in sincerity. Genuine care can't be faked; its recipient senses it deeply. Our Lord Himself demonstrated this attentive compassion, taking notice of those many would overlook and investing Himself entirely in the lives of His disciples.

In a supportive network, space for transparency is non-negotiable. Within the safe confines of trust and acceptance, members can share their struggles without fear of judgment. James instructs believers to confess their sins to one another so that they may be healed—a process made possible only in an atmosphere of respect and confidentiality. Such transparency leads to powerful prayer and intercession as members stand in the gap for each other.

Navigating seasons of hardship and joy together solidifies the ties within a faith community. Friendships forged in the furnace of trials are resilient. They survive and thrive, offering proof to a watching world of the redemptive power of Godly companionship. The words from Ecclesiastes ring true: two are better than one, for they have a good return for their labor. Should one fall, the other can help them up—but pity the one who falls without another to assist them.

One cannot overlook the role of mentorship within the network. Timothy had Paul, Elisha had Elijah—these relationships allowed wisdom and experience to be passed down. Mentors act as anchors, offering guidance through spoken wisdom and the example of their lives. They model what it is to be anchored in the Word and sponsored by grace, thus empowering others in their spiritual walk.

Empathy is the golden thread that ties the hearts of believers together in support. It allows us to rejoice with those who rejoice and mourn with those who mourn. When one part of the body suffers, all parts suffer; when one is honored, every part rejoices. This empathetic bond reflects the character of Christ, who, though in the form of God, did not consider equality with God something to exploit but emptied Himself for the sake of humanity.

Serving each other within this network is another avenue to demonstrate Christ's love. When Jesus washed His disciples' feet, He exemplified servanthood's humble heart. To follow His model is to seek opportunities to aid and uplift others, affirming their value and worth in the Kingdom of God. Through such acts of service, the network becomes supportive and transformative.

To sum up, a supportive network in the life of a believer is vital for spiritual health and growth. It manifests the Kingdom's interdependent relationships, requiring humility, vulnerability, and a commitment to one another's well-being. This network is not an end but a means by which believers can live the grace-filled, Word-centered life God desires.

In a world filled with isolation and individualism, the Church stands as a beacon of community, drawing its strength not from the similarity of its members but from the unity bestowed by the Spirit. Each one's faith journey is personal and communal, and it is within a supportive network that this paradox finds its beautiful balance.

Through every trial and triumph, the Christian network testifies to the goodness of a life bound by the Word and coursing with grace. This network is a testament to the transformative power of Gospel living, a signpost of the Kingdom to the beleaguered souls seeking refuge and hope. It embodies the very essence of embracing community through grace.

Encourage One Another in Faith

In the symphony of our lives as believers, encouragement plays a vital melody that resonates through the heart of the community. As we journey together, intertwined by our experiences and bound by our collective hope, we must uphold and fortify each other's faith. In Hebrews, we're reminded to consider how we may spur one another on toward love and good deeds, not giving up in gathering together, as some are in the habit of doing, but encouraging one another—and all the more as you see the Day approaching.

Living in a gracious community involves a conscious effort to uplift our brothers and sisters. Each of us carries the power to inspire courage, kindle hope, and reinforce faith. Encouragement is more than mere words; it's the extension of God's grace towards one another. When we affirm and support each other, we reflect God's endless encouragement towards us, fortifying the weary and uplifting those burdened by trials.

Encouragement isn't limited to praising successes; it also entails walking alongside others during their most trying times. Sometimes, the simple act of being present and listening with empathy ignites encouragement within a struggling soul. The gentle whisper that says, "You are not alone," can bring immeasurable comfort and strength. Life in Christ's body is akin to a tapestry, woven together by threads of individual stories, each supporting and enhancing the beauty of the whole.

To encourage faith means to echo the truth in the Word of God, providing reminders of God's promises and His unwavering faithfulness. It's through scripture that we find the ultimate source of encouragement. Scriptures are laden with assurances that God is our refuge and strength, always ready to help in times of trouble. When we embed these truths in our hearts and share them with others, we act as vessels of God's grace, encouraging others to steadfastness and perseverance.

Fostering an environment of encouragement requires intentionality. It can be as deliberate as setting aside time to build others up or as spontaneous as seizing the opportunity to speak life into someone's situation. We ought to be alert to the needs within our community, ready to offer a word of hope or a gesture of kindness that signifies solidarity and shared faith.

This nurturing engagement fuels growth within the body of Christ. The apostle Paul vividly describes the church as a body with many parts, each indispensable and designed to work in unison for the good of the whole. As each of us operates in our God-given gifts and calls, encouragement becomes the lubricant that ensures the smooth functioning of this divine machinery. It facilitates harmony and effectiveness in our collaborative pursuit of God's purposes.

Prayer, too, is a cornerstone of encouragement. When we intercede for one another, we acknowledge our dependency on God's sovereignty and invite His intervention in our collective and individual struggles. There's profound power when we stand in the gap for our brothers and sisters, bringing their needs before the throne of grace with ardor and faith.

But why is encouragement so crucial? Life inherently presents challenges that can erode our faith and cause despair. Encouragement anchors us to hope. It reminds us that our current trials are not the story's end but steppingstones to a more remarkable testimony—a reminder of our victory in Christ.

Let's not forget the impact our words and actions have on the lives of those within our sphere of influence. With wisdom and sensitivity, encouragement should be tailored to meet individuals where they are. Some may need gentle reassurance, while others require bold exhortation. Discernment is necessary to understand and administer the correct form of encouragement that will enlighten and not discourage.

Furthermore, we must recognize that encouragement is a two-way street. As much as we give, we must also be open to receive. Pride can often hinder one from accepting encouragement, but it's essential to humble oneself and acknowledge that we all need support. In doing so, we allow others to fulfill their role within the body of Christ and provide the encouragement we need to endure and overcome.

In practicing encouragement, it's critical to maintain a forward-looking perspective. Encouragement is about dealing with the present and pointing towards a future grounded in God's promises. It marries the present realities with the certainties of our hope in Christ, providing a balanced view that motivates and uplifts.

Moreover, the practice of encouragement must never be tainted by insincerity or performed as a mere duty. It should flow from a genuine concern for the well-being of others, mirroring the heart of Christ, who consistently offered encouragement throughout His ministry on earth. When our encouragement stems from a place of love and authenticity, it can transform hearts and situations.

As members of the body of Christ, we must cultivate a culture within our communities that prizes encouragement. This means breaking through the barriers of isolation and creating channels of communication that allow the free flow of improvement. It involves setting aside personal agendas to focus on the needs of others and fostering an atmosphere where each individual is esteemed and valued.

In conclusion, encouraging one another in faith is a divine directive that carries profound significance in our lives as believers. When enacted with intentionality, discernment, and genuine love, encouragement becomes a potent force that strengthens the bonds within our communities, equips us for the battles we face, and propels us toward our eternal destiny in Christ. Let us, therefore, be vigilant in this high calling, knowing that as we pour into others, we are serving God Himself and contributing to the glorious work of His kingdom.

Chapter 10:
Grace in Service and Ministry

Opening ourselves to the divine inspiration that breathed through the apostles, we now turn our focus to serving others with a heart ignited by grace. It is in the purely selfless act of giving — not seeking recognition or recompense — that grace manifests its true power in the realm of service and ministry. As vessels of this incomparable love, our aim is never to garner attention but to deflect it back to the Source, allowing His light to pierce the darkness through our works. Grace equips us with a humility that banishes every shade of pride, calling us to kneel as servants before a world in need.

In this profound service, varied as the colors in a tapestry of light, we uncover the beauty of God-given gifts, each one purposed for the edification of the Body. Radically different abilities come together, as intended by the Creator, to weave a pattern of care that blankets the world with tangible expressions of grace that speak louder than words. This chapter invites us to serve with a heart washed clean of ego, attuned to the whisper of the Spirit guiding us to love in a manner not just heard, but seen and felt.

Serve with a Humble Heart

In the journey of service and ministry, a cornerstone often unheralded is cultivating a humble heart. Humility is not about thinking less of oneself, but rather thinking of oneself less, guiding one's actions to be not for self-promotion but rather for the greater glory of God and the edification of others. As servants and stewards of the divine grace we have received, humility must be the soil in which our service is rooted.

To serve with a humble heart is to recognize that our ability is a gift from God, not something of our own making. It's to understand that our role in the Kingdom is not to elevate ourselves but to lift others in prayer, encouragement, and practical service. This pattern is shown throughout the Scriptures, where true greatness is consistently marked by servitude and humility.

Consider the example Jesus Himself set; the King of Kings stooped to wash His disciples' feet, demonstrating that the highest form of leadership is found in serving others. This wasn't just a one-time lesson in humility—it was a call to a life characterized by the same attitude. Instead, he, who had every right to demand service, became the Servant of all, leaving an indelible mark on the fabric of Christian service.

It should be noted, too, that humility isn't an advocating of weakness. In truth, it requires immense strength to put aside one's ego, to serve others with no thought of reward, and to face possible derision without the armor of arrogance. Yet, this strength isn't our own—it is derived from a deep-seated faith in God, from where we draw the power to serve humbly.

A humble heart is also a listening heart. It's open to the guidance of the Holy Spirit and sensitive to the needs of others. Such a heart is attuned not just to words but to the silences between; it seeks to understand more than to be understood. In this receptivity, we become better servants and witnesses to the grace we've graciously given.

Furthermore, humility allows us to cherish unity over personal preference. In a world that exalts individualism, it's a bold stance to value the collective good of the body of Christ above personal fame and satisfaction. Humility does not demand uniformity but harmonizes diversity, ensuring that multiple gifts work together for the common good.

Service with a humble heart also means forgiving others and asking for forgiveness, for it recognizes human fallibility, including our own. We must be quick to extend grace, aware that we, too, need grace in abundant measure. Serving is, after all, not about perfection but about love in action, love that covers a multitude of sins.

Let's not forget that humility is a safeguard against the snares of pride that can afflict those in service and ministry. Pride, that insidious root of all sorts of evils, finds little room to grow in the garden of a humble heart. It's in the moments when we're tempted to bask in the accolades of our service that we must return to our knees, the position of ultimate humility before our Maker.

And so, a service life is not a stage for our greatness but a platform to reflect God's glory. Our deeds, whether seen or unseen, whether lauded or overlooked, offer a sweet aroma to the heavens when carried out in humility. It's not the magnitude of the service that matters but the magnitude of the love and humility within it.

In embracing this call to humility, we must also be patient. The kind of humility that truly enhances service and ministry doesn't blossom overnight. Like all virtues, it's cultivated over time, often through trial and error and continuously leaning on God's grace. Patience with ourselves and with others is an essential ingredient in this process.

We serve best when we embrace the reality that we are merely vessels of more excellent work. As messengers of the gospel, our aim should be transparency—to let His light shine through us unimpeded by the stains of our ego. When people look our way, our hope should be that it's not us they see—instead, let them discern in us the visage of Christ.

A humble heart also embraces teachability. We should always be willing to learn from God and those we serve alongside. There is wisdom in the counsel of many and the recognition that we don't have a monopoly on understanding or capability. Being correctable and open to guidance is a hallmark of a humble servant.

It's also essential in our service to support our brothers and sisters, acknowledging that the body of Christ is not a competition but a collaboration. Encouraging others in their gifts and callings is as essential as diligently pursuing our own. A humble heart cheers on others without envy or comparison, rejoicing in their successes as if they were our own.

In practical terms, humility in service means being willing to do the tasks that go unnoticed, that aren't rewarded with human accolades, that are often unseen but are no less significant in the Kingdom of God. It's the selfless offering of one's time, resources, and talents, not for fame or acknowledgment but because we understand that is what we are called to do.

As we tread the path of service with a humble heart, we should be diligent in remembering that it is not ours to determine the results of our service. We plant and water seeds, but God is the one who gives the growth. Our responsibility is faithfulness, not the accounting of fruit—that is in the Lord's hands, the very hands that modeled humility unto death on a cross for our sakes.

Recognize the Diversity of Gifts

In the beautiful tapestry of God's creation, variety and diversity are not merely evident; they're central to the masterpiece He weaves within His people. When we turn our gaze to service and ministry, it is essential to recognize and celebrate the myriad of gifts bestowed upon us through the Spirit's generosity. Just as the human body comprises different members, each contributing unique functions for the health and activity of the whole, so too is the body of Christ enriched by the diversity of its gifts.

Each believer has been endowed with gifts that differ according to the grace given to us, and therein lies a profound mystery and practical wisdom for the functioning of the church. We are urged to exercise these gifts with grace and an understanding that no one gift operates in isolation. The teacher needs the exhorter, as the giver needs the leader. Each person, in their unique gifting, contributes to the mission of the church – edifying believers and reaching the lost.

It's through the lens of this diversity that we can see the multifaceted glory of God reflected in His people. Yet, recognizing this variety calls for a heart posture of humility and respect for one and another's distinct role. Comparing gifts or desiring the gifts of others can foster division and discomfort within the body. It's important to embrace one's own gifting, understanding that the smallest function, performed in love, is invaluable in God's kingdom.

We must also be vigilant not to stereotype or box in these gifts. The Spirit can manifest His power in surprising ways, often choosing the unexpected moments or people to demonstrate His grace and power. A gift of prophecy may surface in a teenager as profoundly as in a seasoned preacher, and gifts of healing and miracles can manifest through those whom society might overlook.

Encouragement is a gift that breathes life into the faint-hearted, and it's one that multiple members of the body can share in the practice. Encouragers can identify the flickering wick of one's faith and gently fan it into a flame. Through words of comfort, they reinforce the courage of others to persevere through trials and tribulations.

While some are called to be apostles and prophets, sent forth with messages of deep spiritual significance, others are called to the quieter yet equally vital roles of service and teaching. Teachers, who unfold the mysteries of God through the exposition of Scripture, and those who serve, often behind the scenes, are like the hidden roots that sustain a great tree. Both are essential for the flourishing of God's people.

Giving, leading, mercy—these gifts must not be overlooked in their importance. The givers provide for the needs of the saints and extend hospitality, their generosity acting as a vessel for God's provision. Leaders guide with diligence, and those gifted with mercy act with a cheerfulness that softens the hardest of hearts.

What's more, these gifts are not stagnant; they grow and mature through faithful stewardship and prayerful development. A small seed of a gift, watered by the Word and nurtured through practice, can grow into a mighty tree sheltering many under its branches. As we seek God's direction and refining, He can expand our capacities to serve Him in new and unexpected ways.

Exercising these gifts in love remains paramount. If gifts are misused, operated out of selfish ambition or pride, they can become tools of destruction rather than building. Love is the currency of the kingdom, and it is in love that these gifts find their purest expression and their most profound impact.

Envision a church where each member not only understands their gifting but also fervently supports their brothers and sisters in cultivating their own. Such unity in diversity exemplifies the prayer of Christ—that all would be one, even as He and the Father are one. In this unity, the world sees a glimpse of the divine harmony that characterizes the eternal kingdom.

It's also crucial to appreciate seasons in the context of our gifting. Just as there are seasons of the year, there are seasons in our service to the Lord. A gift might be prominent at one stage of life, then take a subdued role in another. Awareness of God's timing is essential to effectively steward the diverse gifts we've been given.

To further foster the diversity of gifts, we should create environments within the church that encourage exploration and practice. Whether through formal training, mentorship, or simply the freedom to participate in various ministries, we should be given the space to discover and refine the gifts given to us by the Spirit.

Lastly, let's remember that the Ultimate Giver of gifts is God Himself. It is He who decides which gifts we receive and for what purpose they serve in His grand design. Thus, our heart's posture should always be one of gratitude, as every good and perfect gift comes from above, from the father of lights with whom there is no variation or shadow due to change.

In the recognition of the diversity of our gifts, we uncover a more profound mystery—the beauty of God Himself working in us and through us. With every gift acknowledged and appreciated, we don't just see disparate individuals, we witness the body of Christ functioning in harmony, displaying His grace for all the world to see.

Chapter 11:
The Discipline of Gratitude

In the journey through the valleys and peaks of life, the steadying force of a grateful heart serves not only as a beacon of hope but also as a firm declaration of trust in the providence of God. When we weave the fabric of gratitude into the daily rhythm of our existence, we acknowledge the myriad ways in which grace enriches our lives, even in the most mundane moments. It's a discipline, indeed, for it requires intentionality to elevate our gaze above our circumstances, to find the silver linings etched within the storm clouds.

As we cultivate thankfulness, we find our hearts expanding in worship, our eyes opening to the continuous thread of God's benevolence that permeates our stories. This chapter, therefore, is a call to anchor ourselves in gratitude, allowing this virtue to shape our perspectives, guide our reactions, and ultimately, transform our relationships, as we recognize and honor the divine generosity that underpins our every breath.

Foster a Thankful Spirit

Fostering a thankful spirit is akin to tilling the soil of one's heart so that seeds of joy and peace may take root. The practice may seem simple, but it runs deep, challenging our natural inclinations and reshaping our perspectives. To develop a spirit of gratitude, one must often confront the complexities of the human experience, balancing the tension between suffering and blessings.

Thankfulness is not merely a reaction to the receipt of good things; it is a disciplined choice to recognize the value in every situation. Yet, in this pursuit, many find themselves at odds with their circumstances, struggling to summon gratitude amidst trials. This conundrum elicits a question of profound significance: How can we maintain a thankful spirit regardless of our external conditions?

The Scriptures provide a profound insight into this question. The Apostle Paul encourages believers to "give thanks in all circumstances; for this is the will of God in Christ Jesus for you" (1 Thessalonians 5:18). The inclusive term "all" underscores that thankfulness is not contingent upon our circumstances but upon the steadfast character and promises of God.

Gratitude, when woven into the fabric of our daily lives, requires an awareness of the multitude of graces that color our everyday experiences. To cultivate such understanding, a conscious decision to shift one's focus from lack to abundance is necessary – this is the essence of gratitude.

The practice of gratitude begins each morning when one wakes – the simple yet profound act of being alive brings forth the initial spark of thanks. As the day unfolds, every interaction and task, no matter how mundane, carries an opportunity for thanksgiving. Do we recognize the privilege of labor, the laughter of a friend, or the nourishment of food? These are graces undeserved yet freely bestowed.

Delving further into the discipline of gratitude, one finds it requires an acknowledgment of dependence. We are not self-sufficient beings navigating through life's trials alone. Our breath itself is a gift. As we acknowledge our need for sustenance from our Creator, our hearts soften, and a thankful spirit burgeons within us, displacing pride with a profound sense of humility.

In the practice of thanksgiving, repetition is critical. The words of gratitude uttered in prayer, the list of blessings compiled in writing, and the vocal expression of thanks to others – these repeated actions train the heart to seek out and celebrate goodness. Like a well-trodden path, the more frequently we walk in gratitude, the more natural it becomes to our soul's disposition.

Even in suffering, there is a peculiar grace to be found. It may come as the comfort of a friend, unexpected strength in adversity, or character growth through trials. A thankful spirit recognizes that even the darkest times are sovereignly used by God to shape and refine us. In this recognition, gratitude does not ignore pain but finds a more profound sense of purpose.

There is an inherent connection between gratitude and generosity. When one's heart is brimming with appreciation for the grace received, sharing with others becomes an overflow of that gratitude. The thankful spirit finds joy in giving, for it understands that blessings are not solely for personal enrichment but for communal benefit.

Intertwined with the act of thanksgiving is the virtue of contentment. Contentment is learning to be at peace with what one has, knowing that our circumstances, both in plenty and in want, are temporary states in the larger narrative of life. Gratitude anchors us in the present moment, enabling us to find satisfaction amidst the ebbs and flows.

Reflective practices enhance our capacity for a thankful spirit. Contemplating the steadfast love of God, His mercies, and our redemption story can swell the heart with appreciation. These quiet moments of meditation are not merely intellectual exercises but are encounters with the divine that reorient our hearts toward gratitude.

Much like other disciplines of the faith, thankfulness thrives within a community. Shared expressions of gratitude, communal prayers of thanks, and the mutual encouragement to acknowledge God's provision form a symphony of voices lifting praise. Within the body of Christ, the individual's thankful heart is amplified, reverberating through the lives of others.

Gratitude in action is acknowledging that every aspect of our lives is under God's grace. Thus, when we carry out our daily responsibilities with a spirit of thanksgiving, our work is transformed into worship, our interactions become offerings of praise, and our very existence testifies to the goodness of the Lord.

Finally, embracing gratitude is an eschatological act, pointing us toward the ultimate thanksgiving that awaits eternity. As we echo the psalmist's praise, "Give thanks to the LORD, for he is good; his love endures forever" (Psalm 107:1), we anticipate the day when our thanksgiving will be made perfect in His presence.

In conclusion, a thankful spirit is not an accessory to the Christian life; it is its heartbeat. As we persist in the discipline of gratitude, let us trust that our practice will yield an abundant harvest – a life characterized by joy, peace, and a profound sense of God's presence within and around us.

Recognize Grace in Daily Life

In past chapters, we've delved deeply into the many facets of grace and its unmerited favor. Yet, it's critical to our spiritual journey to understand grace from a biblical standpoint and identify and acknowledge its manifestation in the everyday moments of our lives. To cultivate a discipline of gratitude, one must become adept at perceiving grace in the minutiae of our daily existence.

Grace often appears in the simplest of garments, in a stranger's gentle kindness, or in a friend's steadfast love. It's present in the chirp of a bird on a morning's dawn, reminding us of new mercies and beginnings. Recognizing grace is a matter of tuning our hearts to see God's hand in the tapestry of our ordinary days.

Often, we're keen to share grand testimonies of divine intervention, but grace is also the incremental growth we see in ourselves. It's the patience we didn't have, the wisdom gleaned from Scripture applied to a workplace dilemma, or the quiet strength to care for a loved one.

To discern grace, one might start the day in reflection, considering the gifts that cannot be earned: the air we breathe, the life we've been given, and the eternal hope we carry. These are not merely happy accidents but are intentional expressions of God's love toward us.

It's in the provision of daily bread, a job that provides, or even a moment of laughter despite hardships. These instances don't shout with the force of a storm; they whisper with the tenderness of a loving Father, beckoning us to appreciate the divine fingerprints on what we too often consider mundane or ordinary.

In cultivating a discipline of gratitude, prayer is indispensable. In the quiet and honest communication with the Almighty, we begin to frame our minds toward recognition of the small graces. Through prayer, we can ask for the Holy Spirit's assistance in opening the eyes of our hearts to see God's grace woven throughout our everyday experiences.

Another avenue to discover grace is through fellowship and sharing life with others in the body of Christ. Sometimes, others reflect grace to us by offering a word of encouragement exactly when needed or by extending forgiveness when we've gone astray.

The Scriptures provide a reservoir to drink deeply of grace's reality. Stories of Jesus' compassion, Paul's encouragement in tribulation, and the Psalms' raw emotional poetry remind us of the grace that permeates every aspect of human experience, even as it did thousands of years ago.

Grace is also found in our failures and setbacks. Odd as it may seem, in these times when we're most aware of our shortcomings and the consequences thereof, grace stands in the gap. The gentle nudge to get back up again, the absurdity of peace in a tumultuous heart, and the refusal to be defined by our lowest moments are all grace at work.

Serving others selflessly showcases grace in an actionable way. When we leave our comfort zones to bless someone anonymously or commit to a cause that uplifts the downtrodden, we both give and receive grace. Such acts embody the gospel message and mimic our Savior's sacrificial love.

We must also stay vigilant not to ascribe grace only to the positive. Sometimes, it's grace that we find in the discipline of a loving Father, correcting our path for our good. And often, it's through challenges that we are molded into a clearer image of Christ – grace in disguise.

Creatively documenting grace can be a practical method to keep it at the forefront of our consciousness. Keeping a journal, creating art, or even composing a song can help us express our discovery of grace and, in doing so, solidify its presence in our lives.

Recognizing grace in daily life calls for a pace that allows for reflection. In the hustle of our modern existence, it's easy to overlook the divine touches. Hence, finding moments of stillness is critical to developing an eye for grace in the rhythm of the everyday.

As it relates to recognizing grace, the practice of gratitude isn't a passive affair. It demands active engagement, a deliberate pause, and a decision to look beyond what's seen. In this faithful and constant seeking, we see grace for what it truly is: God's ongoing testament of love to His creation.

Thus, let us journey forth with eyes wide open to the grace ever before us, for in it, we uncover the beauty of God's narrative that weaves through each moment of our lives. And let that discovery fuel our enduring song of gratitude in heart and practice as we acknowledge every perfect gift from above.

Chapter 12:
The Leadership of the Word

As we continue to explore the profound influence of Scripture, we discern that the Word not only comforts and teaches but also leads with unparalleled authority. In this chapter we recognize that Biblical leadership isn't simply a matter of wielding power, but an exercise in stewardship, one that marries authority with profound humility. For those called to lead, Scripture offers a blueprint that subverts worldly paradigms, holding up servanthood as its core tenet.

This is the leadership of the Word—a leadership that doesn't lord over the flock but tends to it, nurturing growth through the example set by our shepherd, Christ Jesus. As we delve into the dynamics of such leadership, we uncover the balance and wisdom needed to guide others in truth and love, aiming always to reflect God's grace as we walk the path set before us.

Biblical Guidance for Leadership

The scriptures, replete with wisdom and insight, present a profound blueprint for leadership anchored in servanthood and characterized by grace. In the unfolding narrative of sacred texts, we find leading figures who, though flawed, exemplify God's design for those called to guide and shepherd others.

First, let's consider Moses a figure of humility despite his substantial role. Encountering God in a burning bush, he's tasked with leading the Israelites out of bondage. This illustrates a pivotal leadership principle: actual authority is not self-asserted but divinely commissioned.

In the fabric of Moses's story, we discern that leadership involves intercession. Privy to the Divine counsel, Moses stood in the gap for the people, highlighting a leader's role as an intermediary who pleads for those under their charge.

Another exemplar is King David, who, despite his humble beginnings, was exalted to the highest station in Israel. His leadership teaches us the importance of a heart in tune with God's own—such dispositions foster leaders after God's own heart.

David's penitential psalms reveal that effective leadership acknowledges personal failings. Confession and repentance aren't signs of weakness but strength, establishing a framework for authenticity and transparency in guidance.

The wisdom literature, particularly Proverbs, offers further dimensions to godly leadership. It encourages leaders to seek wisdom fervently, as one would seek treasures. Wise counsel, the fear of the Lord, and understanding are the bedrock of sound decision-making.

But the most perfect example is Jesus Christ, whose very life is the quintessence of leadership. He who came not to be served but to serve encapsulates the heart of leadership—service, a laying down of one's life for others.

Jesus's leadership was marked by compassion and proximity to the needs of people. He touched the untouchable, loved the unlovable, and empowered the powerless. His model teaches us that authentic leaders see and respond to the plights of those they lead.

The apostle Paul's letters are rich with advice for leaders. Timothy and Titus were young leaders under Paul's guidance, receiving instruction on maintaining sound doctrine, facilitating orderly worship, and managing church affairs with dignity.

Paul's qualities for overseers in 1 Timothy 3:1-7 foreground the notion that a leader's character is paramount. Above reproach in conduct, temperate in action, respectable in demeanor, and hospitable in nature—a leader's life must be an open book, inviting scrutiny and emanating the light of the Word.

As outlined in the scriptures, leadership is not about dominion but stewardship. Each one is accountable to God for how they manage the lives and resources entrusted to them. Effective stewardship calls for diligence, faithfulness, and understanding, which honors God and affirms His lordship over all creation.

Crucially, Biblical leadership is rooted in discipleship. The Great Commission, a mandate to make disciples of all nations, sets forth a leader's mission to lead and foster growth, instill knowledge, and replicate character reflective of Christ.

This sacred calling comes with both privilege and price. James cautions that teachers will be judged more strictly. The gravity of this responsibility accentuates the need for leaders to remain humble, always seeking God's face for wisdom, understanding, and direction.

In conclusion, the Word furnishes us with abundant examples and principles for leadership. As we endeavor to lead in any capacity, let's draw upon these Biblical insights—crucibles for cultivating a heart of service, forged under the hammer of God's guidance and shaped by His unending grace.

Walk in Authority and Humility

The delicate interplay between authority and humility is a balancing act that those guided by the Word must learn to navigate. As leaders and stewards of faith, we are called to wield authority and embody humility. The Scriptures, replete with wisdom, grant us the vision to walk this path with discernment and grace. They steer us away from the cliffs of arrogance, guiding us instead toward the fertile plains of servanthood.

To walk in authority, one must recognize the source of their power. For those rooted in the Word, authority comes not from personal prowess or worldly accolades but from an understanding that we are vessels of a higher decree. We lead by a mandate that transcends our capabilities, and to do so effectively, we must constantly align ourselves with divine direction and purpose. However, authority is not to be mistaken for dominion that casts a shadow of oppression; instead, it's a light that guides and empowers others to discern their pathways.

Conversely, humility arises from an acute awareness of our human limitations. It is the embrace of our need for God's grace and the realization that, apart from it, we can do nothing of eternal value. A leader entrenched in the Word understands that humility is the soil in which true wisdom grows and that pride is but a noxious weed that threatens to choke the life out of fruitful endeavors.

Jesus, our paramount example, walked in a perfect synthesis of authority and humility. He spoke to storms with the command of a Creator and yet knelt to wash His disciples' feet with the tenderness of a servant. In His footsteps, we find the essence of authentic leadership—dominion over the chaos of sin coinciding with compassionate service to others.

Authority, when rooted in biblical understanding, carries an inherent responsibility. It is the duty to act justly, to love mercy, and to walk humbly with God. One cannot correctly fulfill such a role without a spirit attuned to servanthood, for scripture consistently lifts the humble and cautions against the exaltation of self.

Holding authority requires that we also cultivate a spirit of empathy. A leader must share in the joys and sufferings of those they lead, always seeking to understand before seeking to be understood. Such empathy is born out of humility and fueled by the love we've first received from Christ.

Walking in authority and humility means daring to subvert these norms in a world that often equates leadership with control and power. It means using our influence to serve rather than be served, leading by example rather than by mandate.

The practical outworking of this balance often looks like seeking counsel and being teachable. A leader who listens acknowledges they don't possess all wisdom. In the multitude of counselors, safety and a well-spring of collective insight can enhance individual discernment.

Furthermore, walking in authority and humility necessitates a willingness to be corrected and to repent. The most outstanding leaders recognize their missteps and are swift to seek reconciliation and restoration, both with God and those they lead.

A relentless pursuit of justice and righteousness also marks the path. Holding the reins of leadership doesn't mean lording it over others but rather advocating for those without a voice, defending the weak, and upholding the cause of those less fortunate.

We must also surround ourselves with people of integrity who will encourage us in our faith walk. Leaders thrive in communities where transparency is valued, and individuals can express their vulnerabilities without fear of judgment.

Lastly, we must nurture a spirit of gratitude to walk in authority and humility. Acknowledging that every victory, every wise decision, and every step forward is a gift from above keeps us grounded in humility, even as we exercise the authority granted to us.

As we continue to grow and assume positions of greater responsibility, let us remember that the core of our leadership must be love—a love that speaks truth but also bends to bind the wounds of those we serve. For in the grand tapestry of God's plan, it is love that covers a multitude of sins, and it is love that ultimately reflects the heart of our Savior.

Thus, the mantle of leadership is worn not as a token of superiority but as a commitment to reflect God's character in every action. In such a way, leaders centered on the Word can truly walk in the tandem grace of authority and humility—never abusing the former, never neglecting the latter, constantly advancing with a clear vision set by divine providence.

May we each strive to be such leaders, understanding that our charge is sacred, our mission profound, and our guide infallible. Let us then proceed with the confidence that comes from being anchored in the Word and resolve to exhibit the grace that has been so lavishly bestowed upon us.

Chapter 13:
The Horizon of Eternity

Emerging from the guidance of the Word on leadership, we're beckoned to lift our eyes to the infinite promise that dawns at the end of life's voyage—the Horizon of Eternity. Amid the turbulence of temporal concerns, it's easy to lose sight of the eternal scope etched into our destiny. However, the fabric of Scripture weaves an undercurrent of perseverance, encouraging believers to anchor their soul's hope in the assurance of what is yet to unfold beyond the veil of this present age.

In this chapter, we'll explore the profound impact of eternal perspective on our daily choices, character development, and commitment to God's mission. As pilgrims journeying through a transient world, let us delve into how the luminous prospect of glory shapes our present reality, not through escapism but by infusing our every moment with purpose, grit, and a divine sense of direction that illuminates even the darkest paths with the inevitable dawn of God's unending day.

Look Forward From Glory to Greater Glory

Within the hearts of those who walk by faith is an indescribable yearning, a longing akin to homesickness for a home not yet beheld, a place beyond the present. This anticipatory desire, solidified by the confidence of what is promised, molds a believer's perspective, giving them a lens through which to view the temporal as but a shadow of the eternal. As believers look forward, they envision the greater glory that is not just a destination but the culmination of God's redemptive work in us.

The anticipation of glory is a beacon of hope that shines steadfastly through the murkiest of life's waters. This hope isn't anchored in fanciful wishes or contrived dreams; somewhat, it is grounded in the confident assurance revealed in the sacred Scriptures, for the text speaks of the glory that awaits the faithful, far surpassing the trials and tribulations of our transient existence.

In this life, followers of Christ confront myriad challenges. The path is rarely smooth; it often leads through the thorny underbrush of hardship and suffering. Yet, buoyed by grace, believers continue to journey forward, not as weary travelers but as expectant heirs of a rich inheritance. The promise of glory instills in us a resilience that defies the frailty of our condition.

Looking forward to glory implies an understanding that the present suffering is a momentary affliction. Believers embrace the conviction that these light momentary troubles are preparing for us an eternal weight of glory beyond all comparison, as though life's pains are the labor pangs heralding the birth of something new and splendid.

While gazing ahead at the promise of glory, believers are called to live in a manner worthy of the calling they have received. This living hope shapes the believer's future and their present actions and attitudes. It clarifies the purpose of our earthly journey, reminding us that every act of kindness, every word of truth, and every deed of faith is a brushstroke on the canvas of eternity.

Through grace, the view of eternal glory has practical implications. It teaches us to hold the things of this world loosely, to see them as temporary tools for eternal purposes. Possessions, positions, and even relationships are given their due significance without becoming ultimate in our affections or aspirations. For where your treasure is, there your heart will be also.

By aligning our will with God's, we find that our deepest desires meld with a heavenly agenda. Love, joy, peace, patience, kindness, goodness, faithfulness, gentleness, and self-control overflow from a spirit attuned to the divine, serving as signposts of the glory destined for the children of God. These fruits are ancillary to the Divine law written upon the heart, the royal law of love, which propels us toward the kingdom to come.

The prospect of glory offers an invitation to let go of past guilt and embrace the transformative power of forgiveness. As God in Christ forgave us, so we are equipped to forgive others, releasing the chains of bitterness that seek to bind our souls. This liberation isn't simply for our benefit alone but reflects the coming glory where love reigns supreme.

In moments of worship and solitude, the heart sings of glory yet to be fully realized. These are tastes of heaven on earth, foretastes of the divine banquet at which the faithful shall sit. Communion with God in the here and now is an entrance into the grand fellowship that awaits, where communion will be unbroken, and joy will be complete.

Indeed, the anticipation of glory should nourish our spiritual vigilance, prompting us to stay awake, be clothed in God's armor, and remain steadfast in the face of adversity. The vision of glory girds the believer with the strength to persevere, fight the good fight, finish the race, and keep the faith inspired by the incorruptible crown to be awarded.

Looking forward to glory also humbles us, for it reminds us that our most significant accomplishments here are but a whisper compared to the thunderous applause of heaven. It is not by our might or power but by the Spirit that we are ushered into the presence of the

Divine, and so we run with perseverance, looking not to our strength but to the author and perfecter of our faith.

The call to look forward to glory is to live with eternity in mind. Christians ought not to be so consumed with the present that they forget their faithful citizenship is in heaven, from which we eagerly await a Savior. This forward-looking mindset guides believers in making decisions, setting priorities, and investing their time, talents, and treasures.

The glory that awaits is shared, not isolated. The community of saints, both present and departed, journeys together in this hope. Thus, the church is not a mere gathering but a foretaste of the heavenly assembly. The unity and love shared among believers testify that we're bound for a place where every tribe, tongue, and nation will glorify God in unison.

As this chapter folds into the next, we hold fast to the glory ahead, allowing it to infuse our everyday lives with purpose and passion. To look forward is to live with conviction, to see through the lens of eternity, and to hold every moment captive to the cause of Christ, for it is in Him that we find the fullness of glory and the assurance of our eternal home.

Eternal Perspective in Present Living

Inspired by a vision of eternity, we are invited to navigate the everyday terrain of our lives from an elevated vantage point. To consider eternity is to look through a telescope; our perspective is broadened, and our perception of time and space is transformed. Just as a landscape changes under the light of dawn, so does our view of life when we reflect upon the endless horizon.

When we truly grasp the concept of eternity, our present actions, decisions, and attitudes align with a narrative much more prominent than our transient concerns. It isn't simply about bracing for a distant future; it's about allowing that future to infiltrate and influence our present moments. A life steeped in eternal perspective is profoundly enriched and fundamentally altered.

Understanding the eternal implications of our earthly journey shapes our priorities. We're not forsaking the importance of our current experiences but enriching them by recognizing they are part of an ongoing story. This connection binds together the fleeting and the permanent, rendering our temporal sufferings and joys meaningful within an infinite context.

The Apostle Paul reminds us to set our minds on things above, not earthly. This divine directive doesn't prompt us to dismiss the world but to live in it with purpose and hope. It encourages us to engage with the world passionately and compassionately, yet not be enslaved by its fleeting pleasures and trials.

How shall we live amidst the paradox of eternity that colors our present? We embody a tension —being in the world, yet not of it— by anchoring our values and behaviors in eternal truths. Our ethics, sense of justice, and even our daily labor take on new weight when viewed against the backdrop of forever.

We forge ahead, not as those without aim, but as travelers informed by the map of Scripture, guided towards an eternal destiny. We strive not for vain outcomes but for treasures that moth and rust cannot destroy. We seek to accumulate this eternal currency with every act of kindness, generosity, and faithfulness.

A perspective infused with eternity also radically reframes our view of time. We become stewards of fleeting moments, investing them with the wisdom that each minute reflects a divine gift and opportunity. Thus, we are called to redeem the time, knowing the days are evil and God's kingdom advances with each tick of the clock.

Living in light of eternity fosters in us a profound resilience. As we encounter life's ephemeral agonies, our gaze rests not on the shadows cast by pain but on the unchanging love of our Creator. This understanding encourages us to comfort others, too, recognizing that our consolation is not an empty promise but a foretaste of heavenly peace.

Eternity casts its light upon our relationships, urging us to love not in shallow bursts of affection but with a deep, abiding love that mirrors God's eternal love. We endeavor to forgive as we are forgiven and to view every soul with the dignity deserving of one fashioned for eternity.

In service and ministry, an eternal perspective grants us steadfastness. Our labor in the Lord is not in vain; even when it seems unnoticed by the world, we trust that every cup of cold water given in His name is remembered by Him, who is eternal.

The hope of eternity also prompts us to witness. We share our faith not as a sales pitch for a temporal product but as an invitation into an everlasting kingdom. We present the Gospel of grace as the doorway to an eternal relationship with the Creator, not simply a ticket to a Heavenly afterlife.

With eternity in mind, we shepherd our resources and talents with prudence. We give, knowing that our investment reaps dividends in a currency that does not fluctuate with market trends but is secured in God's eternal economy.

Finally, an eternal perspective reveals to us the heartbeat of worship. Each moment is an arena for prayer, where mundane activities are transformed into sacred offerings. When we embrace the day-to-day with reverence, work becomes worship, conversation becomes communion, and life becomes a living doxology.

To embrace the present with an eye on eternity is to step into the fullness of life, where every breath carries the weight of significance, and every step is an act of faith. Let us hold fast to this vision, enriching our lives with the wealth of God's timeless truths as we walk the path set before us.

As we close this section, let us carry the eternal perspective into our daily lives. Let this horizon of eternity guide our choices, fill our hearts with hope, and fuel our commitment to lovingly shepherd the world around us toward the enduring grace of God until the day dawns and the morning star rises in our hearts.

Chapter 14:
Unleashing the Power of Testimony

In the quiet spaces of a transformed heart, testimony holds a power that echoes the very essence of God's grace. Having journeyed through the scriptural insights on grace and the Word's leadership, we now stand at the threshold of a profound practice—sharing our personal voyages through trials and triumphs. A testimony isn't simply a narrative; it's a beacon that shines on the truth of transformation, inspiring others to believe that what's possible for one is accessible to all.

When we articulate how the unseen hand of grace has navigated our lives, we offer more than stories—we extend an invitation to see God's faithfulness at work. Testimony bears the weight of experience and the lightness of divine joy, reminding us that our individual tales are stanzas in a much grander song of redemption. In this chapter, we'll delve into the ways we can harness the stirring power of our testimonies to impact lives, enkindling hearts with the fire of hope that God is actively moving in our midst.

Share Personal Stories of Grace

The tapestry of our lives is embroidered with threads of experiences, some tangible, others spiritual, yet all intertwined with the elegance of divine grace. Telling personal stories where grace played the pivotal character can ignite sparks of faith in ways that doctrine alone never could. The concept of grace finds flesh and bones in the sharing of our lives, with all its joys, sorrows, triumphs, and tribulations.

In the journey of faith, every believer has encountered those luminescent moments when grace shone through the ordinary. Perhaps grace was the quiet strength that carried one through losing a loved one or the invisible hand that held back the tide of despair during financial ruin. When we share these intimate narratives, we witness the unmerited favor abundantly poured upon us.

But why, one might wonder, is it so essential to vocalize these personal chronicles? Is it not sufficient to silently acknowledge and thank God for His provision? Scripture encourages us not just to hold on to our stories but to profess them, for "they overcame him by the blood of the Lamb and by the word of their testimony" (Revelation 12:11). Through the sharing of our testimony, we unite the body of Christ, edifying one another and glorifying God.

Consider the woman with the issue of blood, who was healed after years of suffering upon touching the hem of Jesus' garment. Not only was her healing a testament to divine grace but her act of coming forward to tell her story was equally poignant. It wasn't just her courage that captivated her, but the magnitude of her faith, which inspired all witnesses.

As vehicles of God's grace, we mustn't let humility morph into reticence. While modesty is a virtue, silence can deprive others of the encouragement found in our testimonies. In sharing, we testify not to our worthiness but to God's limitless mercy and love. It's essential to recognize that our stories of grace may very well be the key that unlocks faith in someone else's heart.

Let's not forget the impact of authenticity in our testimonies. The authenticity of our stories lends them power. When we recount how we wrestled with doubt, fear, or anger before grace met us, our vulnerability resonates with those fighting similar battles. The reality of grace becomes most potent in the candidness of our narratives.

Sharing our grace-filled stories also serves as a communal reminder of how grace operates outside the confines of merit. The prodigal son's story illustrates this beautifully. It wasn't his repentance that earned his father's forgiveness but the unconditional love that the father had, which mirrored God's grace towards us. Our story could be the reassurance someone needs that grace is not a prize for the flawless but a gift for the wayward and repentant.

To share our stories of grace, we must first be active listeners of others' experiences. There is profound beauty in the reciprocity of sharing and receiving testimonies. As we open our hearts to the wonders that God has performed in our brothers and sisters' lives, we find our faith stirred and strengthened.

Moreover, as we peruse the Word, we find it replete with personal accounts - David's psalms brim with raw emotion, Paul's letters reveal a life radically transformed by grace, and Jesus' parables often reflected the lives of those He spoke to. The Scriptures themselves advocate for the sharing of personal journeys.

Still, one might wonder about the place of stories in a world that seems increasingly skeptical of subjective experiences. Here, the inherent power of shared stories of grace truly shines. A story can transcend intellectual barriers and address the yearning for truth planted within every human soul. It is not that telling our experiences should replace the teaching of sound doctrine. StilStilluld accompany it, providing a relatable context that allows grace to be perceived in its splendor.

When we gather, whether in church halls or over coffee, let us not merely focus on the superficial but delve deeper into the spiritual chronicles that shape us. In sharing personal stories of grace, we foster an atmosphere where the supernatural becomes natural, where divine intervention is expected and celebrated. It allows us to see God not as a distant deity but as an intimate Partner in our daily walk.

The multiplicative effect of shared testimonies is also worth noting. As one share, another is encouraged to voice their own experiences, creating a chain reaction that amplifies God's goodness and grace. Our narratives then become personal milestones and communal monuments to God's faithfulness.

As we contemplate our stories of grace, let us approach with prayerful reflection. Asking the Holy Spirit to guide us in our sharing ensures that our words will be seasoned with sensitivity and a clear purpose. We must seek not to sensationalize or embellish but to convey the objective truth of God's grace as we have encountered it in the cacophony of life's complexities.

In essence, sharing personal stories of grace is not merely a recital of events but a powerful tool for spiritual warfare, a means of evangelism, and a cathartic journey. It fortifies believers, converts skeptics, and, most importantly, ascribes glory where it is due— to the Author of Grace Himself. So, let us be generous with our stories, and in doing so, may we unleash testimony's transformative power.

Impact Lives through Testimony

In the previous chapter, we illuminated the significance of sharing personal stories of grace. We now turn our attention to the profound impact that testimony can have on the lives of others. To bear witness is not merely to recount an event but to speak of the transformation that ensues when the divine threads of grace interweave with the human tapestry of experience.

When one freely shares their journey through the landscapes of faith, from the valleys of despair to the peaks of jubilation, one offers a gift to the listener. This gift carries with it a powerful potential to usher in hope, fortify faith, and draw hearts closer to the truths we cherish. Such is the potency of testimony—its ability to transform lives extends beyond the orator to the attentive ear that seeks understanding.

Consider the diverse ways in which a single testimony can reverberate throughout the soul of a community. It's as if each narrative were a pebble thrown into a pond, ripples reaching farther shores. Testimonies of grace speak of overcoming adversity, healing restored, provision bestowed, and mercy generously given. They stand as living proof of the promises that so often leap from the pages of Scripture into the reality of our daily walks.

These narratives illustrate how tribulations were surmounted through faith, encouraging others who may currently tread similar trials. They serve as beacons of light, revealing that the pathway, though wrought with challenges, leads to a place of victory and peace. Thus, when one shares how they were anchored in the storm through the Word and sustained by grace, it equips fellow sojourners with the resolve to continue their journeys.

Moreover, testimony acts as an agent of unity. Hearing how God's faithfulness has manifested in our brethren's lives binds us in the likeness of shared experiences. Through this, we are reminded that despite our unique paths, we are all partaking in a collective pilgrimage enriched by the same Spirit who gives life to all things.

The transformation testified to is not only spiritual but often practical and tangible. Testimonies can inspire relationship change, where grace thrives and animates forgiveness and reconciliation. They exhibit the potent capacity of Scripture to alter life's daily rhythms, change habits, redirect passions, and elevate sights to higher nobilities.

Empathy is woven into the fabric of a heartfelt testimony. As one recounts their vulnerabilities, struggles, and the subsequent embrace of

God's grace, it generates a profound resonance with those who also know the familiar taste of frailty. It encourages a kindred spirit, fostering in listeners a courageous vulnerability to share their stories, confess their faults, and cleave to the healing and restoring power of grace.

Witnessing the transformation that occurs when one is deeply anchored in the Word likewise reinforces the credibility of Scripture. In a world where many are led astray by fleeting narratives and question the relevance of ancient texts, the incarnate Word, active and effectual in the lives of believers, stands as irrefutable evidence of the Bible's timeless authority and influence.

A testimony validates God's providence and sovereignty. It speaks to His unsearchable ways, and through this, the listener's perspective can shift from doubt to recognition of God working intricately throughout history and in personal lives. In times of social upheaval and uncertainty, stories that affirm God's control comfort and reassure the anxious heart.

As members of the Body of Christ, testimonies evoke our collective calling. They remind us that we are part of a grand narrative, each playing a unique role in God's redemptive plan. They stimulate us to embrace our gifts, to engage fervently in service, and to partake joyfully in the ministry to which we are appointed.

Importantly, testimonies of sinners turned saints serve as tangible outflows of the Gospel message. They personify the act of being born anew, the shedding of the old self, and donning the new. Such dramatic life alterations, when recounted, can captivate and challenge the skeptic, giving substance to faith's claims and making abstract concepts vividly real.

In proliferating testimonies, we participate in a sacred echo of the great cloud of witnesses before us. We join the time-honored chorus that testifies to God's enduring faithfulness across generations. We stand on the shoulders of those who have pioneered the faith and, like manner, carry the torch to light the way for others.

Testimonies thus wield a dual sword: they illuminate, and they evangelize. They build up the Body, encouraging perseverance and the pursuit of holiness, and they reach out to the lost, showcasing the transformational power of grace and truth in a believer's life. This seemingly simple tool is mightily effective in the Kingdom's work.

In light of this, let us be mindful of the power in our stories. Each of us is a living epistle, bearing marks of grace's penmanship. Let us not be reticent in sharing the wonders that God has worked in our lives. Let's be bold to proclaim, educate, and comfort, for in doing so, we embody the living testimony of grace made manifest.

As we reflect deeply on the indelible truth that our testimonies have the potential to impact many lives, we are charged with a profound responsibility and a wondrous privilege. May we each carry forth this blessing, this transformative power of testimony, with steadfast conviction and joy.

Conclusion

This book, "Anchored in the Word and Sponsored by Grace," addresses the essence of substantial spiritual assistance from the Almighty God. In this book, we have unfolded the divine pattern of God's Word and graceful strands within the material design that has gotten us through life's highs and lows. We journeyed through the topics of graciousness and scripturalism that grace our relationships, problems, and calling to become a spiritually mature whole by completing each other using these two heavenly tools.

We can take refuge in the fact that these timeless truths present here will empower us to meet life's challenges. As we continue to serve with humility and love, our hearts are ready to accept the grace current. At the same time, our eyes are pointed toward eternity's horizon, in which hope burns brightly as a promise of future glory for us all.

Basics that serve as the foundation for further study have been addressed through these conversations by looking at how grace and the Word impact all aspects of our lives. These chapters have shown us that these two divine tools help them develop a spiritual maturity symphony that enables people to survive storms in life courageously with certainty and sense.

The conclusive message is that readers can derive comfort from what they learn about life and its pain points in this book. The eternal truths of grace and the compass of the Word bring hope to readers, for they can never abandon their spiritual journey because God will be there every step they go.

Ultimately, this book teaches us how Grace and God's Word change people. As we navigate the peaks and valleys of life, these talks in this book have revealed the divine beauty of God's grace, an unwavering substance that is His Word. Moreover, this message stresses that, as Christians, we should aim to impact those around us through faith, not just ourselves.

Summary of Key Points

In traversing through the explorations of grace and the Word in our lives, we've unearthed profound truths that realign our focus, fortify our faith, and frame our journeys with the resounding assurance only found in divine revelation. The landscape of our discussions has been vast, but herein, we'll encapsulate the pivotal themes that serve as guideposts to the trail we've trekked.

The concept of grace remains a cornerstone of our faith. Grace, as unmerited favor, arrives unsearchably deep and life-transformingly potent. It stirs within us a transformation that redefines our character, motives, and actions. The tales of grace that dance across the Biblical narrative are not merely historical footnotes but living, breathing exhortations that this same grace is at work within us today.

Our partnership with grace is enlivened through faith. A faith that's not passive but vibrant and responsive. It grasps the grace extended and ventures into realms of righteous living and conscientious action, where spiritual growth flourishes and holiness is pursued not as a burdensome duty but as a passionate expression of gratitude.

This journey of faith is inseparable from the Word, the inerrant and sufficient Scripture that serves as both compass and map. In its lines, we encounter God's heart, His vision for His creation, and the wisdom to navigate life's often murky waters. The Bible's robust nature as God's revelation equips us to plumb the depths and scale the heights of spiritual maturity.

Grace and the Word empower us to be agents of transformation in ourselves and our communities. The close-knit fabric of Christian relationships is not without its fray. Yet, grace teaches us the art of forgiveness, and the Word instructs us on reconciliation and love, mirroring the unconditional love Christ has shown us.

As much as the Word roots us in truth, grace teaches us resilience amid adversity. In our weakest moments, grace is the well from which we draw strength, and the Scripture is solace and hope. Trials may buffet our ships, but anchored in the Word, we can weather the fiercest storms.

Grace does not exist to be hoarded. It's to be shared, radiating outward like beams of light breaking through the darkest skies. While grace beckons us to carry its message to the ends of the earth, the Word sharpens our witness tools, enabling us to share its riches effectively and authentically as true ambassadors of Christ.

The transformative journey calls us to reflection; examining our growth is not an exercise in vanity but a means to witness God's handiwork in us. And the charge to abide, to remain steadfast in God's Word and grace, carries with it the promise of a life lived to its fullest potential.

Community plays a crucial role in bolstering our spiritual vitality. In accepting and spurring each other toward love and good deeds, we form a network that sustains us, amplifies our joy, and divides our sorrows. This solidarity is the hallmark of a life steeped in grace and truth.

Service and ministry, catalyzed by grace, allow us to make the intangible love of God tangible. In humility, we recognize and harness the diversity of spiritual gifts, not as a means to elevate self but as a path to glorify the Giver of all good gifts.

Cultivating gratitude, we foster a posture that acknowledges every breath as grace. Recognizing the manifold expressions of grace in the mundane, we discipline our hearts to remain cheerfully attuned to God's perpetual provisions and kindnesses.

In leadership, the principles distilled from Scripture guide us. The call to lead encourages us to walk the delicate balance of authority with the humility of Christ, aware that our ultimate Leader serves not only as our chief example but also as the source of our capacity to lead well.

With our gaze firmly set on the horizon of eternity, the transient nature of our present existence gains clarity. An eternal perspective galvanizes our present living, infusing it with purpose, hope, and an unwavering resolve to pursue what endures.

The power of testimony lies in its ability to present the reality of grace as it manifests in the crucible of human experience. When we share our stories, they echo far beyond the confines of our immediate sphere, impacting lives with the verifiable evidence of grace at work.

The tapestry of themes we've woven from the beginning chapters to this summarizing section provides conceptual understanding and a practical framework. By embodying these truths, we emerge transformed and equipped to navigate life with sure faith, boundless grace, and confidence in an everlasting Word.

Encouragement to Embrace Grace and the Word

As we step into the gentle folds of this concluding section, let us hold fast to the tender invitation extended to each of us: an invitation to fully embrace the grace that has been generously poured out and the Word that stands unwavering through the ages. In this final appeal, should our hearts heed the call, we discover the profound simplicity of living a life richly anchored in divine grace and scriptural truth.

Grasp firmly onto grace with both hands, for it is the unmerited gift that God has lavished upon us. By grace alone, we are propelled through life's storms and brought safely to harbor. For isn't it grace that picks us up when we falter and whispers courage when doubt looms large? Within its embrace, you will find the strength to face even the most daunting days. We have journeyed together through the narratives of grace's indwelling in history, and now it's time for that history to be alive in us.

Simultaneously, let us not forsake the Word, which has been a wellspring of wisdom and guidance for those who have gone before us. The Scriptures, breathing life and truth into our daily walk, equip us for every good work. The Word is more than letters on a page; it is the voice of our Creator speaking directly to the core of who we are, urging us to cast away the shackles of our past and step into the light of understanding.

Indeed, embracing grace and the Word is less about mastering a set of doctrines and more about nurturing a responsive heart. A heart that beats in rhythm with the heart of the Father, seeking to know more of His character, His love, His very essence. As we interact with the sacred texts, let them interact with us—challenging, refining, and shaping us into the vessels of honor intended from the beginning of time.

By weaving grace into the fabric of our everyday existence, we exhibit patience in tumult, kindness in strife, and love in the face of indifference. The grace we have been given for free is the grace we are called to extend to others without prejudice or constraint. This pattern of giving, as we have received, is the hallmark of a life transformed by the mercy of God.

In a similar vein, the consistent meditation on God's Word fosters growth that is both visible and invisible. It transforms the mind and renews the Spirit, enabling us to discern and walk in His perfect will. Therefore, devotion to the scriptures is not a task laden with heaviness but a joyous journey filled with discovery and enlightenment at every turn. We mustn't shy away from delving deep into its riches, for therein lies the power of godly living.

Recognize, too, the profound impact grace and the Word have on our relationships. As we live out these truths, we become bearers of peace and unity, bringing healing where there is hurt and restoration where there is brokenness. Our interactions, built on a foundation of scriptural love, reflect the glory of the One who calls us His children and knits us together in harmonious fellowship.

When the tumult of life rages like an unrelenting storm, grace and the Word become our unfaltering refuge. They instruct us on how to find solace amid chaos, offering solace and resilience. Even as we navigate through uncertain waters, we are bolstered by the promises that ring clear and true, cutting through the clamor of our worries and fears.

As we consider the journey ahead, let us proceed with relentless purpose, upholding the charge to share this grace and Word with those we encounter. Our calling is not merely to hold these treasures close but to offer them freely, to become vessels through which others may also come to know the liberating power contained within.

Do not be disheartened should transformation appear slow or the path seems fraught with obstacles. Embracing grace and the Word is a life-long voyage marked by persistent progression, not instant perfection. Be patient with yourself, and know that with each step you take, the Spirit is at work within, conforming you to the likeness of the Son.

In this sacred endeavor, be assured of the fellowship that surrounds you. You are not alone in this call to abide. The community of believers stretches out its hands, ready to join you in support and encouragement as together you seek to live out the rhythm of grace and truth. Therein lies a stronger bond than the most potent adversary, a unity transcending earthly borders and temporal concerns.

Might we all rise to this noble duty, for in doing so, we bear witness to the transformative power of grace and the enduring truth of the Word. The legacy we leave is not one of fleeting success or earthly accolades but one of enduring faith and luminous hope, which echoes through generations and resounds in the heavens.

Hence, with the close of this volume, I leave you not with an ending but a beginning—the beginning of a fresh commitment to embracing grace and the Word. May these eternal gifts be the daily bread upon which you feast, the compass by which you navigate, the wellspring from which you draw strength, and the anthem you carry forth into the world.

Blessed are those who take to heart the divine consort of grace and the Word, for theirs is a life of abundant promise. As the final words of this text linger, may they be a catalyst that propels you into a deeper, more emotional engagement with the grace bestowed upon you and the Word that lights the path ahead.

Final Thoughts and Blessing

As we draw near to the close of our journey through these pages, let us pause and reflect on the profound truths we have folded into the fabric of our lives. Our shared experience has not merely been about acquiring knowledge but also about allowing the Word and Grace to shape our hearts and minds.

In the quiet spaces of our days, we've explored how grace is not only the foundation of our faith but the very atmosphere in which our souls thrive. We've learned that grace is not a once-given gift but an ever-flowing river, nurturing and sustaining us through all the seasons of our lives.

The Word has stood before us as an unshakeable pillar, a source of revelation, and an anchor for our most tumultuous times. Through the scriptures, we have been equipped, transformed, and renewed, finding wisdom that speaks directly into the core of our being.

Witnessing the transformative power of grace has taught us to forgive deeply, love sincerely, and serve humbly. Our relationships are healed as grace's warm waters soften the hardest of hearts and bridge the widest chasms.

Oh, how the storms have raged, and the waves have crashed against our ship of faith! Yet, anchored in the Word and buoyed by grace, we have navigated through life's fiercest storms, emerging with stronger faith and hope that shines brighter.

In the sharing of the Gospel, in the quiet moments of service and ministry, we have seen the faces of those around us light up with the recognition of grace. Through our testimony and presence, lives are being touched, and choices are shifting toward the Divine narrative.

Remember, it is not our perfection that showcases grace but our imperfections, making room for God's strength to manifest. We are vessels, cracked and flawed, yet grace's light beams out through these very cracks, illuminating the path for others.

Abide in this grace, beloved, for it is your most accurate home. Abide in the Word, for it is your surest guide. As you do so, the fruit of your life will testify to a hope that transcends all circumstances—a hope grounded in eternal promises.

May you be grateful, recognizing every breath as a whisper of grace. Look around you; grace abounds in the mundane and spectacular. It is in every dawn's light and every kind word, nourishing your soul to ever greater thankfulness.

Leadership, too, has been redefined in this grace-filled journey. To lead is to serve; to serve is to pour out the love and wisdom we've received. It's a sacred stewardship asking us to walk with authority and profound humility.

Our eyes are fixed now, not solely on the temporal, but are lifted toward the horizon of eternity. This eternal perspective has reframed our present, filling each moment with purpose and divine potential.

Your story, imbued with grace, now becomes a beacon of hope to those still grappling with the shadows. Your testimony, a powerful melody, will resonate in the hearts of those who hear it, stirring faith where there is doubt and joy where there is sorrow.

And so, as we part ways in this written form, let me impart upon you a blessing: May the richness of God's grace and the truth of His Word be the soil and the sky for the garden of your life. May you grow, flourish, and produce abundant fruit for His glory.

May your heart be courageous, your faith steadfast, and your deeds reflect the One who has called you by name. In every step, may you feel the companionship of grace and hear the whispering guidance of the Word.

Until we meet at the Throne of Grace, go with the assurance that you are loved beyond measure, called to a glorious purpose, and never alone. Amen.

Appendix

In our exploration of God's grace and the transformative power of His Word, an aspect merits special consideration—a dimension where the historical, the spiritual, and the personal intersect. This convergence forms a tapestry of faith woven through the lives of believers across generations. Here, we pause to reflect on the profound legacy that informs our understanding of these eternal principles.

The Scriptures offer a living connection that stretches back to the dawn of creation, chronicling God's magnificent plan for humanity. As we've journeyed through the pages of this material, we've gleaned insights into how grace operates and how the Word stands as our unshakable foundation. This Appendix isn't merely a closing remark but a springboard into deeper waters of wisdom.

We're reminded that while the principles covered in the preceding chapters are comprehensive, they are not exhaustive. The inexhaustible nature of God's Word means that there is always more to discover, understand, and apply to our lives. And grace, in its divine splendor, is as multifaceted as boundless, constantly extending beyond our grasp yet perpetually within our reach.

Indeed, you are not at the end of your pilgrimage; instead, you've arrived at a vista, a place from which to survey the vast expanse that remains to be explored. As your eyes are lifted to the hills from whence comes your help, you can't help but recognize that your help comes from the Lord, the Maker of heaven and earth (Psalm 121:1-2).

Steep yourself, then, in the practice of turning to the annexes of ancient wisdom found in the Holy Scriptures, to the testimonies of saints who've run the race before you, and to the intimate voice of the Spirit that speaks in the quiet moments of heartfelt prayer. Here, in the nexus of past, present, and future, you find the strength to press on, the courage to stand, and the hope that does not disappoint.

May this Appendix A be a testament to the vast reservoir of divine companionship that beckons you to draw from it. Do not see this as an end but as a new beginning, a fresh call to delve into the realms of grace and truth that await you. And as you continue your journey, may you carry with you the everlasting words that have sustained believers for millennia, anchoring your soul and lighting your path.

Recommended Reading and Resources

In our walk with God, it's beneficial to surround ourselves with literature that echoes the truths explored throughout these pages. To assist you in deepening your understanding and to further anchor your life in God's Grace and truth, we've compiled a selection of recommended readings and resources. Engaging with these materials can significantly enhance your spiritual journey.

Firstly, it's essential to establish that the Bible should remain the primary source of spiritual nourishment. The English Standard Version (ESV) and New International Version (NIV) are commended for their balance of readability and faithful translation. Supplementing your study with a robust concordance or a Bible dictionary can prove invaluable for digging deeper.

Consider books that delve into early church history for a historical overview of Christianity's foundations. Understanding the context in which the church was born and grew provides insight into our modern faith and practices.

Christian classics on Grace, such as those written by theologians and scholars who have significantly influenced Christian thought, are next on our list. Works that expound on the doctrines of Grace from various perspectives can give you a multifaceted understanding of this profound topic.

Commentaries on books of the Bible can be constructive. Those by respected theologians offer analysis, historical context, and application that can illuminate the Scripture's intent in ways that a solitary reading might miss.

Spiritual formation is another aspect enriched by literature. Consider works that invite you to practice the spiritual disciplines. These will guide you in prayer, meditation, fasting, and study, creating pathways for Grace to abound.

Do not overlook contemporary authors who speak to the modern heart while deeply rooted in Scriptural truth. Their insights can provide connections that resonate with today's challenges and opportunities for Grace.

Biographies of saints and heroes of the faith serve as powerful testimonies and can encourage and inspire you to live out Grace practically.

For those seeking to understand Biblical leadership, look for books that weave scriptural wisdom with leadership principles, educating and equipping readers to lead with Grace and integrity.

In relationships, texts offering biblical counsel on marriage, parenting, and community fellowship are indispensable. These books will assist in applying Scriptural truths to personal interactions, creating space for Grace to thrive.

Regarding ministry and service, seek materials that motivate and educate on serving within one's capacity while employing one's spiritual gifts. This can result in a more effective, grace-filled service.

Regarding gratitude, devotionals and books that focus on cultivating a thankful heart can transform your everyday perspective, fostering a consistent awareness of God's Grace in all aspects of life.

As we move toward wrapping up this journey, it's essential to have accessible resources that remind us of our eternal home while we navigate our present life. Resources that paint a portrait of Heaven can offer comfort, incentive, and direction.

Lastly, don't forget the wealth of digital resources available. The digital sphere provides immediate access to enriching content from Bible-reading apps to sermon archives, from online courses to podcasts.

This curated selection of recommended reading and resource materials is not to be seen as exhaustive. Instead, it's a starting point, and as you seek, you'll discover additional works that speak to your heart's specific queries and needs. Take these recommendations as companions on your voyage, catalysts for further exploration into the rich landscape of a life anchored in the Word and sponsored by Grace.

REFERENCE LIST

1. Bible Project Team – Sep 18, 2020 "What's the Meaning of God's Grace in the Bible?" Accessed 01/05/2024 | Bible Project ™." Bible Project, bibleproject.com/articles/biblical-grace-and-a-generous-god/.

This online resource provides engaging videos and reading plans that can aid readers in understanding the overarching narrative of the Bible.

2. Bridges, Jerry. Transforming Grace: Living Confidently in God's Unfailing Love. Colorado Springs, CO, NavPress, 2017.

Bridges explore the concept of God's Grace and its transformative impact on believers, providing practical insights for daily living.

3. Blackaby, Henry T, and Richard Blackaby. Seven Realities for Experiencing God. Experiencing God, 2 Jan. 2015.

4. Blackaby, Henry T, et al. Experiencing God: Knowing and Doing the Will of God. Nashville, Tenn., Broadman & Holman Publishers, 2008.

These books from the same authors offer a guide to experiencing God's presence and aligning one's life with His Word and Grace.

5. Bridges, Jerry. The Pursuit of Holiness. NavPress, 19 Sept. 2016.

Bridges addresses the pursuit of holiness, offering a balanced perspective on how Grace and the Word work together in sanctification.

6. Carson, D A. The Gospel According to John. Nottingham, Apollos, 1991.

This commentary provides deep insights into the Gospel of John, emphasizing themes of Grace and the transformative power of God's Word.

8. Foster, Richard J. Celebration of Discipline. Harper Collins, 17 Mar. 2009.

This classic work on spiritual disciplines can guide readers in anchoring themselves in the Word and experiencing God's Grace through intentional practices.

9. Grudem, Wayne A. Systematic Theology, Second Edition; An Introduction to Biblical Doctrine. S.L., Zondervan Academic, 2020.

Grudem's comprehensive work is an excellent resource for understanding critical theological concepts, including Grace and the authority of Scripture.

10. Keener, Craig S. The IVP Bible Background Commentary New Testament. Illinois Intervarsity Press, 2014

This commentary provides cultural and historical context for the New Testament, enhancing the reader's understanding of biblical passages.

11. Lewis, C S. Mere Christianity: A Revised and Amplified Edition, with a New Introduction, of the Three Books Broadcast Talks, Christian Behaviour, and Beyond Personality. New York, Harper One, 2009.

Lewis provides a thoughtful exploration of Christian principles, contributing to understanding faith, Grace, and the Christian life.

12. Packer, J I. Knowing God. Downers Grove, Ill., Intervarsity Press, 1993.

Packer explores the attributes of God, offering profound insights that can enhance the reader's understanding of the Grace and Word of God.

13. Piper, John. Desiring God, Revised Edition. Multnomah, 18 Jan. 2011.

Piper's book explores the pursuit of joy in God, complementing the themes of Grace and the transformative power of God's Word.

14. Strobel, Lee. The Case for Christ. ReadHowYouWant.com, 1 Nov. 2010.

Strobel's investigative approach provides a compelling defense of the Christian faith, touching on themes of Grace and the reliability of the Word.

15. Swindoll, Charles. The Grace Awakening: Hope Again; Simple Faith. Dallas, Word, 1999.

Swindoll's book delves into the concept of Grace, offering practical applications for living gracefully.

16. Whitney, Donald S. Spiritual Disciplines for the Christian Life. Colorado Springs, CO, NavPress Publishing Group, 2014.

Whitney's book is a practical guide to spiritual disciplines that can aid readers in anchoring themselves in the Word and experiencing God's Grace in transformative ways.

www.ingramcontent.com/pod-product-compliance
Lightning Source LLC
Chambersburg PA
CBHW031433270326
41930CB00007B/685